Digital Dialogues 1: Textiles and Technology

Special issue edited by
Janis Jeffries

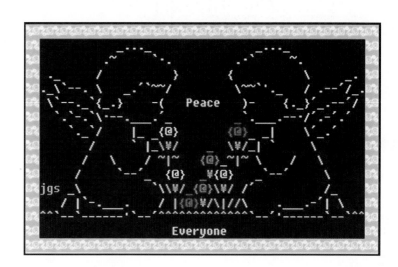

Textile

EDITED BY
PENNINA BARNETT,
JANIS JEFFERIES
AND DORAN ROSS

THE JOURNAL OF
CLOTH AND CULTURE

VOLUME 2
ISSUE 3
AUTUMN 2004

ORDERING INFORMATION
Three Issues per volume. One volume per annum. 2004:
Volume 2

ONLINE
www.bergpublishers.com

BY MAIL
Berg Publishers
C/O Extenza-Turpin Distribution (Customer Services Dept)
Pegasus Drive
Stratton Business Park
Biggleswade
Bedfordshire SG18 8TQ
UK

BY FAX
+ 44 (0)1767 601640

BY TELEPHONE
+ 44 (0)1767 604800

For Enquiries
email subscriptions@turpinltd.com

ENQUIRIES
Editorial: Kathryn Earle, Managing Editor,
email kearle@bergpublishers.com

Production: Ken Bruce,
email kbruce@bergpublishers.com

Advertising: Amelia La Fuente,
email alafuente@bergpublishers.com

SUBSCRIPTION DETAILS
Free Online Subscription for Print Subscribers.

Full color images available online.

Access your electronic subscription through
www.ingenta.com or www.ingentaselect.com

Institutional base list subscription price:
US$160.00, £100.00

Individuals' subscription price: US$65.00, £40.00

Berg Publishers is the imprint of
Oxford International Publishers Ltd.

AIMS AND SCOPE

Cloth accesses an astonishingly broad range of human experiences. The raw material from which things are made, it has various associations: sensual, somatic, decorative, functional and ritual. Yet although textiles are part of our everyday lives, their very familiarity and accessibility belie a complex set of histories, and invite a range of speculations about their personal, social and cultural meanings. This ability to move within and reference multiple sites gives textiles their potency.

This journal brings together research in textiles in an innovative and distinctive academic forum for all those who share a multifaceted view of textiles within an expanded feld. Representing a dynamic and wide-ranging set of critical practices, it provides a platform for points of departure between art and craft; gender and identity; cloth, body and architecture; labor and technology; techno-design and practice—all situated within the broader contexts of material and visual culture.

Textile invites submissions informed by technology and visual media, history and cultural theory; anthropology; philosophy; political economy and psychoanalysis. It draws on a range of artistic practices, studio and digital work, manufacture and object production.

SUBMISSIONS

Should you have a topic you would like us to consider, please send an abstract of 300–500 words to one of the editors. Notes for Contributors can be found at the back of the journal and style guidelines are available by emailing fhowlett@bergpublishers.com or from the Berg website (www.bergpublishers.com).

ISSN: 1475-9756
www.bergpublishers.com

Contents

EDITORS

Pennina Barnett and **Janis Jefferies**
Department of Visual Arts
Goldsmiths College
University of London
New Cross
London
SE14 6NW
UK
p.barnett@gold.ac.uk
j.jefferies@gold.ac.uk

Doran Ross
UCLA
Fowler Museum of Cultural History
308 Charles Young Drive
Los Angeles CA 90095-1549
USA
dross@arts.ucla.edu

TEXTILE: VOLUME 3 ISSUE 1

Digital Dialogues 2: Textiles and Technology

Special issue edited by Janis Jefferies

This exciting special issue investigates digital textiles and represents a pioneering collection of digital work by artists, computer scientists, mathematicians, psychologists, literary and cultural theorists.

Contents include:

Structure of Vagueness - Lars Spuybroek

'Crafting' 'Computer Graphics': A Convergence of 'Traditional' and 'New' Media - Jane Harris

International Collaborative Digital Decorative Design Project - Elaine Polvinen

Electronic Textiles: Wearable Computers, Reactive Fashion and Soft Computation - Joanna Berzowska

Mistaken Ancestry: The Jacquard and the Computer - Martin Davis and Virginia Davis

Intimate Textiles - Ingrid C. Bachmann

Fashion as Aerial: Transmitting and Receiving Cyborg Culture - Adam Swift

March 2005 128pp, colour illus
PB 1 85973 769 2 £15.99 $24.95

free p&p* when you order at www.bergpublishers.com. Also available at booksellers or by telephone: +44 (0) 1202 665432, +44 (0) 1767 604951 or +1 888 330 84767 and Fax + 44 (0) 1202 666219, +44 (0) 1767 601640 and + 1 800 672 2054.

Berg Publishers
First Floor
Angel Court
81 St Clements Street
Oxford OX4 1AW
UK
Tel: +44 (0) 1865 245104
Fax: +44 (0) 1865 791165
www.bergpublishers.com

Letter from the Editors

This is a significant moment in the study of textiles. Radically new technologies are emerging that change both our notions of textile production and our ways of understanding textiles. Conversely, these technologies are themselves informed by the possibilities afforded by a broad range of textile practices. This in itself should surprise nobody—textiles and technological invention have often gone hand in hand—but it does raise fascinating and fundamental questions about textiles and new technologies. *Textile: The Journal of Cloth and Culture* is devoting the first two in its series of special issues to critical writing that addresses these questions. We have sought contributions from a broad swathe of practices. This is the first textiles-orientated publication to incorporate ideas by artists, computer scientists, mathematicians, psychologists and cultural theorists.

Among these practitioners is a new type of multi-disciplinary worker or collective: the artist as researcher, participating at the same time in artistic practice and the development of technologies that are shaping our society,

pioneering research in the development of technologies. A new generation of artists are researching and functioning within a computer-mediated culture. How their work unfolds will become a crucial part of our cultural heritage. That this work is often done in partnership with engineers and scientists is reflected by the number of papers in this volume that are written by multi-disciplinary teams. That these collaborations are fruitful is evident in the range of papers and their implications for art and for technology.

For example, the technologies of the hand—the hand tool, mechanical devices, the computer and digital processes—affect the ways in which we perceive, process and respond to information. These technologies are growing in importance in computer sciences and their development is fundamentally influenced by textile practice. For instance, consider the work being done by artists and designers in the area of reactive clothes: "second skins" and aesthetics surfaces that can adapt to the environment and to the wearers. These clothes enable

Janis Jefferies is Professor and Head of Visual Arts and Director of the Constance Howard Research and Resource Centre in Textiles at Goldsmiths College. She is an artist, writer and curator, and one of the founding editors of the Journal.

Robert Zimmer is Professor of Computing and Head of the Computing Department at Goldsmiths College. He has been a researcher in mathematical foundations and applications of computing for twenty years.

They are also joint Directors of the Goldsmiths Digital Studios, which is a multi-disciplinary research and post-graduate teaching centre spanning work in Computing, Arts, and Cultural Processes.

Textile, Volume 2, Issue 3, pp. i–iv
Reprints available directly from the Publishers.
Photocopying permitted by licence only.
© 2004 Berg. Printed in the United Kingdom.

people to express aspects of their personalities, their needs and their desires.

Partially spurred by these technologies, computer scientists and technologists are investigating the developments and improvements to the quality of the human—computer "touch and feel" interface for computer systems. The research involves probing the inner working of hands; applications include accessing work that is too precious to touch and too fragile for public display within a museum context, and improving interpersonal communication.

Because the technology and its use as an artistic medium have evolved in tandem, the combination has encouraged a great number of remarkable and remarkably fruitful collaborations among artists, technologists, scientists and social scientists. The essays in the two special issues enrich our understanding of creativity and innovation, taking up new lines of inquiry, defining new kinds of research questions, and producing new epistemological models. Andrew Hutchinson in a private communication states that "one of the problems of working in this area, new textiles/active textiles, is that it is so new, so little has been done, and to some extent, the scholarly work is still in the stage of obvious description of practicalities."

The processes of collaborative working and research inquiry underpin several interdisciplinary projects by artists, designers, computer scientists and mathematicians and also underlies many of the contributions to this issue (Vol. 2, Issue 3) and the second (to be published in 2005 as Vol. 3, Issue 1). This introduction, for example, is written jointly by an Artist/Theorist and a Computer Scientist. Collaborative working is a key theme. For example, the essay by Sushil Bhakar, Cheryl Dudek, Sylvain Muise, Lydia Sharman, Eric Hortop and Fred Szabo (Vol. 2, Issue 3), which explores Interactive Grammar Systems for Generative Design, is also done by a multi-disciplinary team. In that paper, computational, grammar-based methodologies are applied to the surface designs of cultural artefacts, notably Congolese Kuba cloth. Pattern recognition is a key in their work. A fascination with pattern emerges as another unifying theme in the collections of essays published in both issues. Pattern—generally characterized by rigorously repeated motifs—is the embodiment of order. In Elaine Polvinen's account of her "International Collaborative Digital Decorative Design Project" with colleagues in Beijing and Taipei, pattern and decoration are interconnected through computer-aided design and student-centered industry and education projects (Vol. 3, Issue 1). In Kerstin Kraft's essay, "Textile Patterns and Their Epistemological Functions" (Vol. 2, Issue 3), another way of looking at the significance of textile patterns is proposed and the cultural implications discussed. A techno-morphological description focuses on textile production processes. Her conclusion that formulating the epistemological functions of patterns will support the interface between cultural and natural sciences connects to the research findings outlined by Bhakar *et al*.

Another way of thinking about pattern is to draw on those qualities that might unsettle or disturb an obsessive practice or engagement. In ""If You Have a Lot of Clutter it Messes up the Popup": The Pursuit of Good *Gestalts* in an Online Folk Art" (Vol. 2, Issue 3), Brenda Danet draws on a database of some 6,000 images captured online. Her paper analyzes the visual form of images and identifies nine strategies that the players employ to pursue good *gestalts*. Danet explores how the strategies are expressed in image form and finds that the pursuit of good *gestalts* leads to pattern and symmetry, especially mirror or bilateral symmetry. The connection between the concept of *gestalt* in psychology and the psychology of art is supplemented with material from interviews with participants.

Cathy Treadaway's essay, "Digital Imagination: The Impact of Digital Imaging on Printed Textiles" (Vol. 2, issue 3), also uses an interview format. Her research into textile artists and designers based in the USA and Europe who are using digital imaging in their creative practice has contributed to her paper through informal interviews, personal correspondence and case studies. Her findings reveal that future developments in computer interfaces and humanization technology will provide even greater opportunities for the creative exploitation of digital imaging technology by printed textile practitioners. The theme of new hybrid craft practices and the opportunity for collaboration through the sharing of digital imagination is pursued by Jane Harris in "'Crafting' 'Computer Graphics': A Convergence of 'Traditional' and 'New' Media" (Vol. 3, Issue 1). The categorization of materials as either "natural" or "synthetic" may also define positive and negative attitudes toward the concept of 3D computer graphic origination. Harris describes her experience of combining "making" skills with computer use. She argues that a unique screen-based language, which is based on material and craft-based skills, finds a new context in the field of 3D computer graphics. The "hand made" working process contrasts with the "man made" workings of digital media. The relationship between the two kinds of workings can be much more intricate and complex than we tend to think, as pointed out by Martin and Virginia Davis in "Mistaken Ancestry: The Jacquard and the Computer" (Vol. 3, Issue 1). Sadie Plant noted that the textile arts preceded and prefigured the computer age: "Weaving was already multimedia," she writes in *Zeros and Ones: Digital Women and the New Techno Culture* (1997: London, p.65). Martin Davis is an eminent computer scientist and Virginia Davis is an internationally recognized weaver. Together they argue that a jacquard loom is no more like a computer than is a piano player, which also used punched holes as an input device. The theme of pattern re-emerges as the pattern threads for a woven textile are mechanized.

A second theme that runs through both issues is that of a "second skin." For Jane Harris, the second skin of cloth and its relationship with the body is evocative and beguiling. Cloth is a material that challenges 3D computer graphics imagery, due to the mathematical complexity of "rendering" this relationship. In "Super Cilia Skin: a Textural Interface" (Vol. 2, issue 3), Hayes Raffle, James Tichenor and Hiroshi Ishii (from the MIT media Lab, Tangible Bits group and Design and Computation, School of Architecture and Planning, respectively) investigate new multi-modal computer interfaces that utilize gesture and the sense of touch to improve personal communication. Super Cilia Skin is an interactive membrane that couples tactile-kinesthetic input with tactile and visual input. As they observe, "like cloth, Super Cilia Skin is designed to engage and sense touch and dynamically move its surface. This is something that traditional textiles cannot do." The dynamics of architectural skins is taken up in Lars Spuybroek's paper, "The Structure of Vagueness" (Vol. 3, Issue 1). His explanation of the analog computing of Frei Otto and its relationship to textile construction provides a grammar of textile as organic form that becomes tectonic and almost a smart fabric in itself.

The final theme is that of smart fabric, also referred to as electronic textiles, animated or intelligent textiles. Their close relationship with the field of wearable computers provides many opportunities for research and collaborative working. Joanna Berzowska writes about her experience as a designer/electrical engineer in "Electronic Textiles: Wearable Computers, Reactive Fashion and Soft Computation" (Vol. 3, Issue 1). She takes a close look at technology for electronic textiles and explores pragmatic applications for electronic textiles, including military research into interactive camouflage and textiles saturated with nanorobots capable of healing wounded soldiers. At the other end of the spectrum, she notes work being done by artists and designers in the area of reactive clothes: "second skins" that can adapt to the environment and to the individual. Anne Farren and Andrew Hutchison's contribution to Vol. 2, Issue 3, "Digital Clothes: Active, Dynamic, and Virtual Textiles and Garments" reads Berzowska's (and Harris') work within the context of conspicuous consumption and the maturing of a field in which revolutionary technologies and bio-feedback sensing are merging with textiles, complex patterns and wearer/end user response.

In Adam Swift's "Fashion as Aerial: Transmitting and Receiving Cyborg Culture" (Vol. 3. Issue 1), the spacesuit is the vehicle for transmitting messages that feed into, and draw from, social and cultural archives. "Second skins" contribute to a highly complex meaning system in which the concept of to and fro transmission and reception is exemplified by the sign of fashion as Aerial. As Ingrid Bachmann maintains in her essay "Intimate Technologies" (Vol. 3, issue 1), textiles continue to be at the forefront of innovation in the aerospace industries. In her presentation of her research trip around a number of textile laboratories in the United States,

Bachmann raises some disturbing questions as to our complex relationship to human, animal and machine life, not least through the growing field of bio-materials; for example, a hybrid of synthetic textiles and a pig's heart valve.

The essays in these two special issues show how new forms of textiles are providing challenging opportunities for people making the technologies; the technologies are providing new ways of creating and engaging with textile culture in the broadest sense. Digital dialogues enhance our understanding of the world, giving us new insights into cultural production and new forms of interaction. "The computer has developed into a versatile tool for modelling systems that reflect our idea about how the world is organised ... Part of the early work in any medium is the exploration of the border between the representational world and the actual world."[1] Cloth uniquely floats across borders of all kinds, conjuring patterns of textual details in the material world and the world of the screen.

Janis Jefferies and Robert Zimmer
London,
September 2004

Note

1. Janet H. Murray, *Hamlet on the Holodeck: The Future of Narrative in Cyberspace* (New York: The Free Press, 1997), p. 92 and quoted in Barbara Layne's essay, "Migrant Textiles: Burdens, Bundles and Baggage," *Re-Inventing Textiles Vol. 2: Gender and Identity* (Winchester: Telos Art Publishing, 2001).

"If You have a Lot of Clutter it Messes up the Popup": The Pursuit of Good *Gestalts* in an Online Folk Art

```
<sam`>  §ℝº˘ºℝ§ℚ§ℝº˘ºℝ§ℚ§ℝº§ℝº˘ºℝ§ℚ§ℝº˘ºℝ§ℚ§ℝºℝº˘ºℝ§ℚ§ℝº˘ºℝ
<sam`>  ¥
<sam`>  ¥        ,\/~~~~
<sam`>  ¥        |  ---,
<sam`>  ¥        `~,  '
<sam`>  ¥        \_|\_\
<sam`>  ¥         \,_|
<sam`>  ¥          ,/
<sam`>  ¥       /ℚℚ _/
<sam`>  ¥       ℚℚ '
<sam`>  ¥      /ℚℚ /
<sam`>  ¥     ℚℚℚ \
<sam`>  ¥     ℚℚℚ |
<sam`>  ¥     `ℚℚ |
<sam`>  ¥      ℚℚ |
<sam`>  ¥      ℚℚ, \
<sam`>  ¥      `ℚℚ, ~\
<sam`>  ¥      ℚℚℚ,
<sam`>  ¥       `ℚℚℚ_,---:::::::=
<sam`>  ¥      ,/~~_---'
<sam`>  ¥       ~`  ~~_/'//
<sam`>  ¥         /' /'|  `ℚℚℚℚℚ,,,,,ℚℚℚℚ  | \..
<sam`>  ¥                   `ℚℚℚℚℚ
<sam`>  ¥
<sam`>  §ℝº˘ºℝ§ℚ§ℝº˘ºℝ§ℚ§ℝº§ℝº˘ºℝ§ℚ§ℝº˘ºℝ§ℚ§ℝºℝº˘ºℝ§ℚ§ℝº˘ºℝ
```

Abstract

This article discusses image form in a computerized text-based art used as a means of real-time communication on Internet Relay Chat (IRC). IRC art developed from ASCII art. The analysis draws on a large database of images captured from an IRC group called "*rainbow*." Evidence is presented for the thesis that creating, playing, and viewing images with certain formal characteristics are a means for the players to strive for, and play with a sense of closure, completion, or perfection. The art also expresses participants' desire for *en*closure, for community. To pursue closure is to pursue *good gestalts*. Nine strategies for the pursuit of good gestalts are identified, including framing and filling the space, cultivating pattern and symmetry in images, especially bilateral symmetry, and avoiding multistable designs. In many respects images resemble traditional embroidery, weaving, rug-hooking, and quilting. However, the ephemerality of this group-based art is novel.

BRENDA DANET

Brenda Danet is Professor Emerita, Sociology and Communication at the Hebrew University of Jerusalem, and a research affiliate in Anthropology, Yale University. The author of *Cyberpl@y: Communicating Online* (Berg, 2001, companion website http://atar.mscc.huji.ac.il/~msdanet/cyberpl@y/), she is researching art and aesthetics online, multilingualism on the Internet, and poetic communication in early medieval Japan. A previous paper on IRC art appeared in *Textile* 1(2), 2003. With Susan C. Herring, she edited "The Multilingual Internet: Language, Culture and Communication in Instant Messaging, Email and Chat," *Journal of Computer-mediated Communication* 9(1), 2003.

Textile, Volume 2, Issue 3, pp. 226–255
Reprints available directly from the Publishers.
Photocopying permitted by licence only.
© 2004 Berg. Printed in the United Kingdom.

"If You have a Lot of Clutter it Messes up the Popup": The Pursuit of Good *Gestalts* in an Online Folk Art

Introduction

This article discusses a form of computerized text-based art displayed on Internet Relay Chat (IRC) as a means of real-time communication.[1] In existence since 1996, this art is an elaboration of an older computerized text art, ASCII (*AS-kee*) art—images created with typographic symbols on the computer keyboard.[2] IRC art is shared: players who are not artists themselves use images created by others when interacting online.

This article presents evidence for the thesis that *creating, playing and viewing images with certain formal characteristics are a means for the players to strive for, and play with a sense of closure, completion, or perfection*. To pursue closure is to pursue *good gestalts*. My title comes from a comment by a Canadian housewife nicknamed ‹kiera›,[3] who says that when creating images, she avoids making her nick (nickname) visible, hiding it in offline coding of images. Her comment aptly illustrates players' and artists' preoccupation with good *gestalts*.

My hypothesis is psychological in nature, focusing on processes of perception and cognition, and on image form. Because images are displayed in a social context, I argue that formal aspects also have important connections with the social nature of communication. Creating, playing, and viewing images with certain formal characteristics are also a means to strive for *enclosure*—for a sense of belonging, for *communitas* (Turner 1969, 1977). Thus, the connection between "closure" and "enclosure" is not merely etymological, but *empirical*. The art encodes the players' aspirations.

Introducing *Rainbow* and its Art

This ethnographic, interpretive research draws on six years of participant observation of a channel (chatroom) on the Undernet (one of the major networks of IRC), called *#mirc_rainbow—rainbow*, for short.[4] Some 5,000 images were captured online; I documented another 1,500 from sets distributed to the players. This article focuses primarily on formal analysis of images, but also incorporates materials from online interviews with thirty-six "ops"—operators, individuals who help run the channel,[5] most of whom are also artists, the ops' mailing list, memoranda from group leaders, and email exchanged with participants.

Figure 1 introduces basic features of *rainbow* art and communication. The group's current leader, ‹sher^›, the group's most admired, most prolific artist and an Illinois housewife, has arrived. Nine players greet her. Nicks of all participants are displayed at the left, as in verbal chat, corroborating that images are a form of text. After three players have greeted ‹sher^› via images, she types, "evening all :)."[6] Greetings culminate in ‹Nik^›'s display of a customized nick file ‹sher^› had designed for herself. We see that communication is more visual than verbal. The art serves as a language of communication, used interactively in real time, and is entirely ephemeral.[7] It is brilliantly colored,[8] and contains play with pattern and symmetry, and with typographic symbols, both those of plain text and "extended ASCII"[9] characters. About half the images are figurative "drawings," and the other half abstract.

Most players are American, from the South, West, and Southwest, though there are also participants from other countries. Most are of blue-collar background, and have a high-school education. About 60% are women, and 40% men, ranging in age from teenagers to people in their seventies, with most in their thirties to fifties.

The Notion of *Gestalt* and Text-based Art

Theoretically, this study builds upon the notions of *closure* and *gestalt* in psychology. The idea of closure in relation to perception originated in *Gestalt* psychology,[10] and was applied to the study of decorative art by the art historian

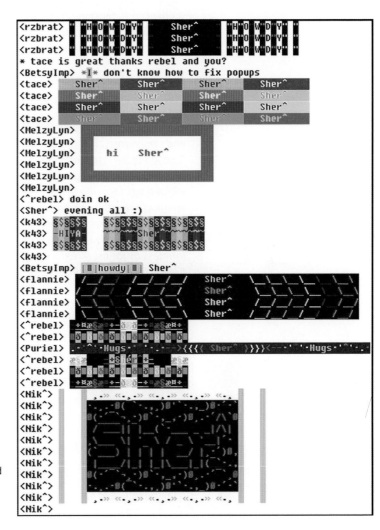

Figure 1

‹sher^›, *rainbow*'s leader, is greeted by nine players. Sixth image by ‹tesla›, last image by ‹sher^›, others, unknown.

E. H. Gombrich (1984). The notion of *gestalt* pertains to our tendency to perceive a stimulus as "whole" even if some portion of it is absent, or to prefer wholes to stimuli that are less than whole. A basic assumption of *gestalt* theory is that people naturally strive for "good *gestalts*." A *gestalt* "is a whole, a new kind of organization with qualities and properties of its own which neither reside in the parts nor can be reduced to them" (Kreitler and Kreitler 1972: 82). *Gestalt* theory contends that stimuli that are unorganized are experienced as tension-producing, whereas organized stimuli are experienced as tension-reducing.

The art of primitive peoples consists mainly of good gestalts, characterized by simplicity, closure, regularity and symmetry … it is this function of the visual arts—the presentation of good gestalts— which lends meaning to the image of the artist as a god or magician who lures order out of chaos and vanquishes the formless by forms. (Kreitler and Kreitler, 1972: 91; emphasis added)

"Good *gestalts* are usually characterized by regularity, symmetry, inclusiveness, unity, harmony, maximal simplicity, and conciseness" (Kreitler and Kreitler 1972: 83). They can be both simple and complex.

Figure 2 distinguishes three groups of *gestalts*. The first row contains simple good *gestalts*, the basic geometric shapes—the circle, triangle, and square. The second group are complex but not good *gestalts*. The eye has difficulty integrating these stimuli because there is no perceptible organizing principle uniting their components. Last are good *gestalts* even though they are complex. Although they are more elaborate, the eye easily takes them in, and does not experience tension while perceiving them because they are highly organized.

The vast majority of IRC images are good *gestalts*. Most abstract images are simple, rather than complex, good *gestalts*. Even irregular figurative drawings offer relatively good *gestalts* because of other features contributing to their visual organization, such as the demarcated space containing them, and the border or frame surrounding them.

Both ASCII art (Figure 3) and IRC art depend for their effects on processes in the psychology of perception. If one views an image too closely, one pays attention to individual typographic symbols more than to the image. When viewing images, the eye "smoothes out the edges" of the letters and other symbols producing their outline or shape. The better the ASCII artist, and the more skilled the choice of symbols, the easier it is to see it as a good *gestalt*.

The relatively small size of *rainbow* images within the mIRC window and computer screen facilitates seeing them as wholes. Images are tiny compared with paintings on a wall. No matter how large the screen, the IRC window contains twenty-three lines. Thus, only images of twenty-three lines or less can be taken in as wholes. Most images are far smaller— shorter—than this. "Popups," the

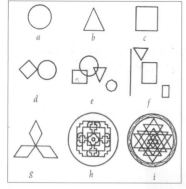

Figure 2
Good and not good gestalts. a–c, Simple good gestalts; d–f, complex but not good gestalts; g–i, complex good gestalts. Source: Kreitler and Kreitler (1972), Figure 4.8.

Figure 3
An ASCII art image of a devil, artist unknown. Christopher Johnson's ASCII Art Collection, http://www.chris.com/ascii/.

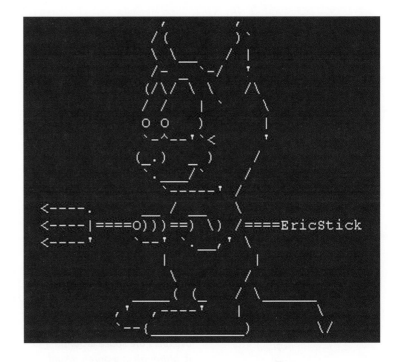

players' term for three- to five-line images (Figure 1) are very popular because they facilitate sharing the visual "floor." Perceived smallness enhances a sense of control and coherence. Among collectors, miniatures such as thimbles and Chinese snuff bottles are popular "because smallness facilitates taking in the whole *gestalt* at once" (Danet and Katriel 1989: 268). The same is true for IRC art, I suggest.

Via play with image form, *rainbow* players conjure order out of chaos, and seek good *gestalts* in a variety of ways, many of which are not mutually exclusive. Figure 4 identifies nine strategies that players employ in the pursuit of good *gestalts*.[11] Some involve extensions or elaborations of perceptual processes in pre-IRC forms of text-based art, or folk and decorative arts. Others are unique to IRC.

Framing and Filling

The first two strategies in Figure 4 are to create, play, or view images with *demarcated space defining them*, and with *filled spaces*. These strategies tend to go together, and

are instances of two fundamental principles of design:

... any hierarchical arrangement presupposes two distinct steps, that of framing *and that*

- Create, play, or view images having clearly demarcated spaces
- Create, play, or view images having filled demarcated spaces
- Create, play, or view images containing pattern and symmetry
- Experience fragmented images as wholes
- Display whole images without interruption
- Play or view sequences of images with common formal features
- When creating images, avoid extraneous material that could spoil a good gestalt
- When creating images, avoid multistable designs
- When choosing ASCII portrayals of animals and people to adapt for IRC, give preference to designs portraying them at a distance

---

Figure 4
Nine strategies for the pursuit of good gestalts in *rainbow* art.

of filling. *The one delimits the field or fields, the other organizes the resultant space. Where the design is applied to a given support, being drawn or painted on a surface, ... the framing grid and the filling motif together constitute the ornament. (Gombrich 1984: 75)*

Demarcating the Space

The most fundamental act in creating any *rainbow* image is demarcating the space it occupies. The psychologist of art Rudolf Arnheim observed that

An animal painted on the wall of a prehistoric cave is essentially unrelated to what occupies the space around it, although in a purely visual sense the paleolithic artist may display some sensitivity to the distribution of shapes on a surface... But as soon as art undertakes to show man in his world, it must show him in space; and to show him in space, a definite delimitation is almost indispensable. (Arnheim 1982: 43)

The art historian Meyer Schapiro (1994) also noted that prehistoric cave paintings were executed on rough, undefined surfaces, adding that we take for granted the rectangular form of the sheet of paper and its arbitrarily defined surface. The invention of the smooth prepared field accompanied the development of polished tools in the Neolithic and Bronze Ages. Over time, "through the *closure* (italics added) and smoothness of the prepared picture surface, often

with a distinct color of the reserved background, the image acquired a definite space of its own" (Schapiro 1994: 3). When demarcating the space around an object, the image maker often locates it in its center. "When stationed in the middle it has another quality for us than when set at the side" (Schapiro 1994: 12).

From ASCII Art to IRC Art

There is a fascinating recapitulation of these fundamental processes in computerized text art. ASCII art images are invariably *without* an explicitly demarcated rectangular space surrounding them, and are often strung together additively. In contrast, images created or adapted for IRC usually include an explicitly demarcated rectangular space. If, unusually, the background has not been colored, images appear to float in the channel window; the boundaries of the grid are invisible.

Framing and Filling: Chronology of an Image

I believe that it is not by chance that when the image of a cute devil in Figure 3 was adapted for IRC, it changed over time in this respect. The version in Figure 3 probably predates the World Wide Web (1992), and may have been created in the 1980s or earlier. Figure 5 displays two adaptations of it for use on IRC. The one on the left was captured in August 1997, the one on the right in February 1999. As in Figure 3, the boundary of the left image is still merely an artifact of my screen capture; the background had been left undemarcated and unfilled, and is white because

Figure 5

Two transformations of an ASCII art devil for IRC. Left image captured August 1997, IRC artist unknown; right image captured February 1 1999, "Fire and Ice" challenge show, adapted by <NightRose>.

no background color had been specified.

In contrast, the version on the right has a boundary demarcated by the IRC artist and an elaborate border, used by me for the screen capture. The background has been filled in with black, the color most used for this purpose. Gombrich's framing and filling are absent in the first IRC version, but present in the second. Increasing technical skill and newer programming options may in part account for these changes. However, it is my belief that the latent pursuit of good *gestalts* motivated them, and that it is not chance that the right image is the later one.

Whatever the explanation regarding this motif, *the overwhelming majority of images captured have clearly demarcated boundaries*, not a function of the screen capture. Additionally, *the space within nearly all images is filled*—either with solid color or with repeated typographic symbols. It might seem trivial to pursue closure by merely filling a space. In research on the phenomenology of collecting I discovered that collectors of all ages take great pleasure in it. For example, a young collector of stickers enjoyed filling the doors of her wardrobe with them. An adult collector of antique travel books to the Holy Land enjoyed sitting opposite his filled shelves, and contemplating how his collection filled them (Danet and Katriel 1989). IRC artists share with many collectors and decorative artists *horror vacui*, "the urge ... to go on filling any ... void" (Gombrich 1984: 80).

Borders and Frames

In Gombrich's (1984) sense, "framing" refers to delineation of the structure or scaffolding on which the object is built. In Western artistic tradition, however, "frame" refers conventionally to the metal or wood structure that encloses an object such as a painting hung on a wall. The frame enhancing the demarcated space is a much later development, though it too is very old. Schapiro (1994) places its arrival late in the second millennium BC, noting that a "framed picture appears to be more formally presented and *complete* and to exist in a world of its own" (Schapiro 1994: 7; italics added).

Since ASCII art lacks demarcated boundaries, it naturally also lacks borders or frames.[12] In contrast, most *rainbow* images have frames or borders, focusing additional attention on the image. Figure 6 displays a variety of borders or frames in *rainbow* art. Most contain systematically repeated typographic symbols; two consist only of solid colors.[13]

In eight examples the border is merely superimposed on the black background of the image, though it is usually prominent because of the use of contrasting color, its width (number of repeated typographic symbols), or the use of solid color only. The contrast between border and field is especially great when there are

Figure 6
Types of borders in *rainbow* art.

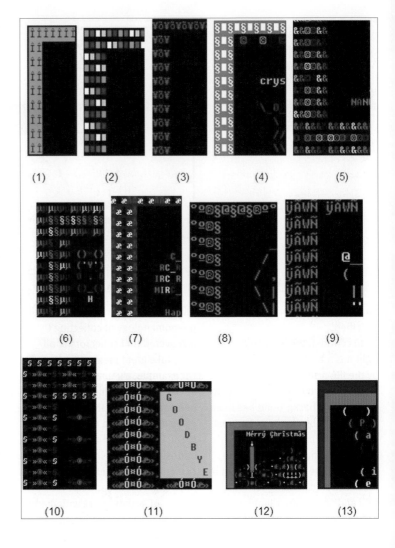

double borders (example 13).
The functions of these borders
resemble those of picture frames:

> No matter what its appearance,
> the frame is always a
> conventional sign indicating
> that what it surrounds is
> out of the ordinary. It marks
> the boundary within which
> something "aesthetically
> important" takes place,
> something that "has no

> practical value." It is artificial
> and pure, and seeks nothing
> beyond its own aesthetic worth.
> (Traber 1995: 226)

In Ortega y Gasset's poetic
articulation

> ... a frame is not the wall ... but
> neither is it ... the enchanted
> surface of the painting. As the
> frontier for both regions, the
> frame serves to neutralize a brief

strip of wall. And acting as a trampoline, it sends out attitude hurtling off to the legendary dimension of the aesthetic island. (Ortega y Gasset 1986: 24)

Borders in *rainbow* images have a quasi-magical function similar to that of traditional embroidery or other decoration on the edges of costumes. What is inside the border is not only enchanted, but *protected*:

> ... evil spirits likely to attack the body are kept out by decorative devices at every edge and opening. From Asia to Western Europe embroidery is commonly placed encircling the neck, along hem and cuff, around pockets and also at buttonholes. Seams are closed with decorative stitchery and certain vulnerable places carry heavy embroidery... Even when they cover much of the garment these areas of embroidery never intermingle but are always clearly defined. (Paine 1990: 133)

Ethnographic research in the 1990s on folk dress in Europe and Asia Minor (Anatolia) supports this view (Welters 1999).

Pattern and Symmetry
The third strategy to pursue good *gestalts* (Figure 4) is *to create, play and view files containing pattern and symmetry*. There are many ways to do this, not necessarily mutually exclusive. *Rainbow* images are extremely rich in pattern and symmetry.

A pattern can be defined as a design composed of one or more motifs, multiplied and arranged in an orderly sequence, and a single motif as a unit with which the designer composes a pattern by repeating it at regular intervals over a surface. The motif itself is not a pattern, but it is used to create patterns. (Phillips and Bunce 1993: 7)

"Symmetry ... is one idea by which man through the ages has tried to comprehend and create order, beauty, and perfection" (Weyl 1952: 5). There is symmetry in leaves, snow crystals, and the human face and body, the bodies of animals and insects, many public buildings, furniture, etc. It is especially common in the art of pre-literate societies, and in traditional arts and crafts such as quilting and weaving the world over.[14]

Magic, Pattern, and Symmetry
One of Gombrich's teachers, Emanuel Loewy, had proposed that an apotropaic function could account for the purpose and origin of most if not all decorative motifs (Gombrich 1984)—that is, decoration is to ward off evil. Sheila Paine adds that embroidered pattern, particularly geometric pattern, is "deemed effective against evil spirits," and "the force of a pattern is strengthened by doubling or repeating it" (Paine 1990: 140). Among the Ainu on the island of Hokkaido, men wore decorated robes while hunting or participating in

religious rituals to keep evil spirits at bay.

> Strong, web-like motifs served to ward off evil spirits and were laid out symmetrically to protect all parts of the body evenly. Decoration was focused on the hem, upper back and front and sleeve openings to prevent evil spirits from entering at vulnerable points. (Jackson 1997: 30)

Similarly, in Palestinian embroidery, the chest panel on women's traditional dresses is the most elaborately embroidered because the chest is considered the most in need of protection from evil spirits (Amir 1977: 13).[15] Summarizing recent research on folk dress in Europe and Anatolia, Linda Welters writes:

> Visually complex patterning is ... thought to prevent evil spirits from inflicting harm on an individual. For example, the evil eye becomes confused by looking at shawls with complicated borders, such as the Slovakian plachta ... or the demon's attention is diverted from a woman's beauty by the long, multilayered fringes of her folk dress. (Welters 1999: 8)

Four Basic Symmetry Operations
Mathematicians have identified seventeen different forms of symmetry in two dimensions (Stevens 1984).[16] Each involves different combinations of four basic symmetry operations (Figure 7).[17]

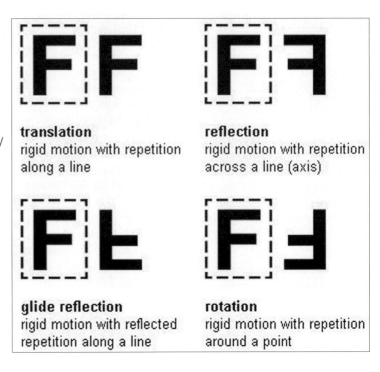

Glide Translation

In the first operation, *translation*, or *glide translation*, as it is sometimes called (upper left, Figure 7), a unit is moved along a line. "An image has translational symmetry if it can be divided by straight lines into a sequence of identical figures."[18] This type of symmetry characterizes border patterns in many ethnographic and decorative arts, and recurs in *rainbow* borders, as in the first example, Figure 6, where a single typographic character is repeated. It also occurs within the field in figurative *rainbow* images. In Figure 8 a motif of seven clover flowers is repeated.

Reflection: Bilateral Symmetry

The second symmetry operation is *reflection*, in which the unit is moved along the line but reversed (upper right, Figure 7). This produces bilateral symmetry, the best known, most easily identified type of symmetry, especially appealing to the eye because it creates a spontaneous impression of balance, harmony, and order (Gombrich 1984; Kreitler and Kreitler 1972). When an image contains this type of symmetry, it is easier to take in details away from the central axis via peripheral vision:

Take a succession of...
signs, such as the following
alternation between repeated
brackets and the letter O:
(((((O(((O((O(O(((((O(((O((O(O.
It takes a moment to see the
underlying rule of diminishing
numbers of brackets and to spot
the redundancy.

Figure 8
Glide translation of an asymmetrical figurative motif by Joan Stark, *rainbow* artist unknown.

But if we do not repeat but reverse the sequence, the impression of palindromic regularity is immediate: (((((O(((O((O(OO)O))O))))O)))) (Gombrich 1984: 126)

Gombrich adds,

... the role of peripheral vision in the global impression of bilateral redundancy ... helps to explain why we rarely notice minor deviations from symmetry, unless we are set to discover them ... Only when our attention has been drawn to ... irregularities do we find it hard to disregard them. (Gombrich 1984: 126–9)

The rest-inducing quality of bilateral symmetry becomes clear when it is violated. The Norwegian artist Edvard Munch painted a portrait of his sister in which he placed her slightly off-center. Schapiro wrote of this painting:

When stationed in the middle [the image] has another quality for us than when set at the side... A visual tension remains, and the figure appears anomalous, displaced ... this appearance may be a deliberately sought expression ... the tendency to favor an off-axis position has been noticed in the drawings of emotionally disturbed children. (Schapiro 1994: 12)

Perfect or near-perfect bilateral symmetry—vertical or horizontal or, both—is extremely common in *rainbow* images. Figure 9 contains striking, perfect vertical bilateral symmetry. An op called ‹tlc-› displayed it to honor his wife and fellow op, ‹mistydawn›. Much more rarely, bilateral symmetry is on the diagonal (Figure 10).

A special case of bilateral symmetry is *heraldic* symmetry. In ancient Assyrian and Egyptian art "paired animals [are] arranged symmetrically to either side of an intervening central element" (Riegl 1992 [1893]: 241). Sometimes,

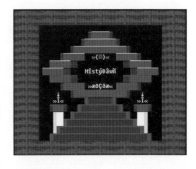

Figure 9
An abstract image with perfect vertical bilateral symmetry, by ‹tlc-›.

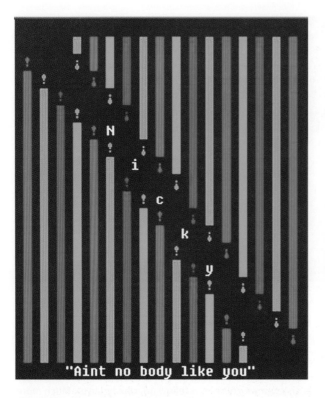

Figure 11
Heraldic symmetry in *rainbow*
art, original design by Joan
Stark, adapted for IRC by
<nuffers>.

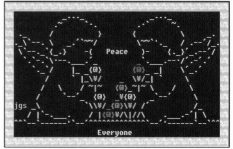

Figure 10
Diagonal bilateral symmetry, *rainbow*
artist unknown.

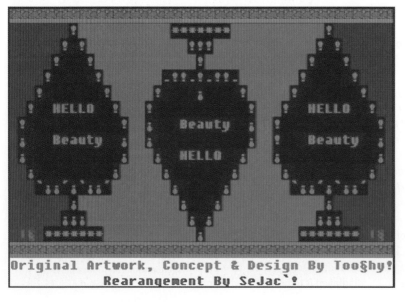

Figure 12
An image containing
glide translation, rotation
symmetry, and double
bilateral symmetry, adapted
by <Sejac> from a work by
<TooShy>.

pairs of human beings are displayed this way too. Often, the head of the animal is portrayed frontally, the body in profile. In other instances the animal or person is in full profile. Similar motifs appear in folk art of many kinds, including embroidery, weaving, and hooked rugs.[19] *Rainbow* artists also create images containing heraldic symmetry (Figure 11).[20]

Glide Translation and Rotation Symmetry

Although individual typographic symbols cannot be reversed or rotated in this medium, larger motifs can be rotated. However, it is difficult to turn an entire motif upside down. Unusually, Figure 12 contains rotation symmetry and glide translation. Two vertical "spades" surround a third, in which the unit has been turned

180°. In addition to the bilateral symmetry of the spade itself, the entire image is bilaterally symmetrical.

Repetition of Words

Another way to create pattern is to repeat words, contributing to semantic redundancy and transforming words or letters into an eye-catching visual pattern (Figure 13). Most commonly,

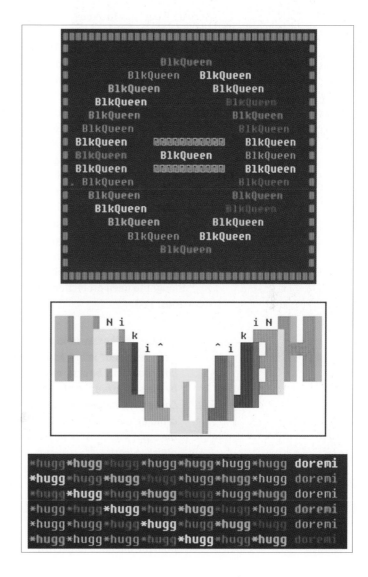

Figure 13

Repetition of words to create visual pattern; first image modified by <sher^>, original IRC artist unknown; second image, artist unknown; third image a script by <patches>.

recipients' nicks are repeated, whether vertically, horizontally, on the diagonal, or even in a circle. Sometimes the words "hello" or "hug" are repeated, with or without repetition of the recipient's nick too.

Interlace Designs

Interlace designs, familiar from many magical and religious contexts, recur in *rainbow* art. Interlace is a form of "braid," twist or "knot" in which elements are intertwined, producing a near-three-dimensional effect. This motif has been identified in Neolithic pottery (Wilson 1994), Roman art (Trilling 2001), Islamic art, and Anglo-Irish manuscript illumination (Gombrich 1984; Grabar 1992; Wilson 1994).[21] Gombrich (1984: 263) cites Hildburgh's (1944–5) suggestion that in folk belief knots and mazes are considered to offer protection against evil influences. Knots are traditionally associated with doors, windows, religious symbols, and the beginnings and ends of books—areas or objects thought to need protection (Trilling 2001: 135).

> *A curse or other spell was often "secured" with a knot, and could only be disarmed by physically untying it. Conversely, magical protection could be built into a knot, which the aggressor must untie for the attack to work...*[22]
> *Defenses against the evil eye are traditionally eye-catching or confusing or both, on the principle that the gaze can be neutralized by deflecting it from the intended target to a*

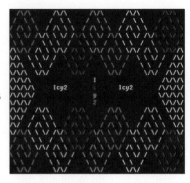

Figure 14
An interlace design by <diedra>.

> *seductive ... or visual puzzle. (Trilling 2001: 135)*

Viewing the design in Figure 14, the eye struggles to establish the nature and location of the basic U-shaped unit *vis-à-vis* its "other half." Are the two "locked together?" Is one U-shape simply "sitting" on a square of the same dimensions? Which one is "on top?" Such images signal "It is safe within this protected space; no harm can come to you!"[23]

Pure Geometric Shapes

We have seen that because ASCII art images are fundamentally geometric, they are necessarily regular rectangles, even if the underlying grid is invisible, and that usually, boundaries are explicitly demarcated. Other geometric shapes, such as triangles, circles and hexagons, occur too, within explicit rectangles or with the underlying rectangular grid suppressed. We already encountered a circle in Figure 13.[24] Often a symbol of unity and perfection, the circle is among the most ancient known human symbols. It appeared in prehistoric rock paintings, and has been in use in ideographic systems of writing for more than 5,000 years (Liungman 1991: 274). One thinks also of the mandala:

> Mandala is a Sanskrit word meaning magic circle, and its symbolism includes all concentrically arranged figures, all radial or spherical arrangements, and all circles or squares with a central point. It is one of the oldest religious symbols ... and is found throughout the world. (Fordham 1953, cited in Gombrich 1984: 246)

Unique among geometric shapes, the circle has infinite axes of symmetry. Not surprisingly, it appears in many folk traditions. It is a potent symbol "of the cosmic force of the sun and moon and of the motion and rejuvenation of the wheel ... [and] offer[s] protection from evil spirits" (Paine 1990: 141). Circles in *rainbow* images express the players' longing for wholeness, unity, and coherence.

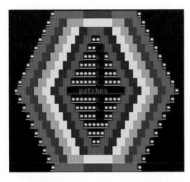

Figure 15
A hexagonal design by <kymmy>.

In the hexagon in Figure 15 the artist has made a mistake: the black central "cross" is askew because she allotted an even, rather than an odd number of spaces for the widest internal line. But this "mistake" does not prevent us from experiencing the image as symmetrical.

Pattern and Symmetry in Borders: A Closer Look

There are interesting types of pattern and symmetry within borders too. The first two examples in Figure 6 repeat only one typographic character; the next four are created with two characters. Visual variety is introduced through judicious use of color as well as repetition of symbols. The third example employs the characters ¥ and ö. Because both symbols are symmetrical, and because two incidences of the yen symbol surround the other symbol, we have bilateral symmetry within the border, at least in its vertical parts. The vertical part of example 4 also appears symmetrical; the eye does not notice that the § symbol is not reversed when repeated.

Example 7 employs three extended ASCII characters; examples 8 and 9 contain four. In the latter example, the word "yawn" is repeated, playing with the tension between word as text and as image. With visual wit, this border has been coordinated with the field of the image (Figure 16). This practice is by no means new. In a fifteenth century prayer book created for Anne de Bretagne, Anne is shown at prayer in the field; the border consists of repetitions of

Figure 16
Witty coordination of field and border, artist unknown.

the letters of her name, A N E.[25] There are more elaborate *rainbow* borders too (examples 10, 11, Figure 6).

Compartments and Lattices

Yet another variant of pattern in *rainbow* art is the organization of motifs into compartments and lattices, "usually ... a means of highlighting or framing design units ... Compartments ... announce the beginning of a new theme within an all-over design or ... underpin a single motif repeated throughout the field" (Purdon 1996: 44). It is particularly common in multiples, images in which nicks of two or more recipients can be inserted. In Figure 17 there is no lattice—a horizontal and vertical grid imposed on the design—though other *rainbow* images do have them.

Fragments and Wholes

Often, the flow of images online is often anything but smooth. What the players call "picture collisions" is quite common. In Figure 18 <carMAN> is trying to play the file he uses when logging off. His

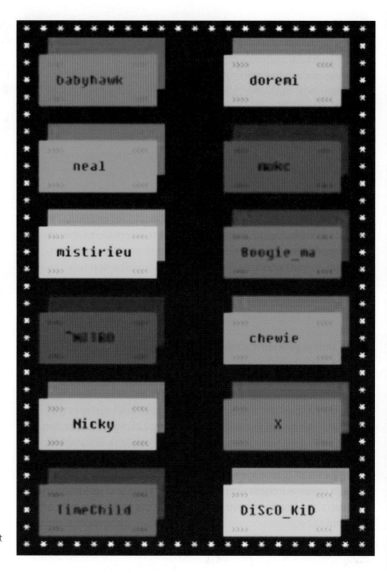

Figure 17
A multiple with compartments, artist
unknown.

image is interrupted by another one, and by bits of text.

There are several reasons for the frequency of "spoiled" images. First, if two or more players hit "Enter" at the same time, the server attempts to display all at once. Second is the problem of "flooding": playing large files can cause players to be "bumped" from a channel, leaving images only partially displayed. Technical improvements increasingly solved this problem. The comings and goings of players, acknowledged by the software in one-line messages, often interrupt displays. By activating certain commands, knowledgeable players can suppress these messages. However, text typed by others in the channel cannot be suppressed.

Figure 18
Replaying a file after a collision.
Image by <carMAN>.

Figure 19
Sequences of images of the same
form, first image, script originally by
<Dwight>, reworked by <DuKeCuPiD>;
second script by <patches>.

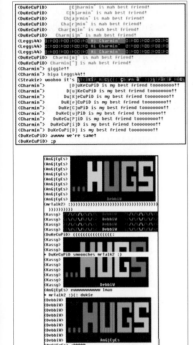

Rarely does one view a sequence of five or more uninterrupted images, as in Figure 1. In short, an important strategy for the pursuit of good *gestalts* is to manage to play and even to view whole files without interruption (strategy #4, Figure 4).

Figure 18 is especially interesting because not <carMAN> himself, but *another* player, <patches>, succeeds in displaying the entire file for him! Whereas he had added the word "all," so that the file would read "cya later ... all," <patches> made the file say "cya later carMAN." Appreciatively, he types, "LOL patches."

It was a great surprise to me to discover that hundreds of images in my database were fragmented in this manner. Eventually, I realized that my surprise was an important clue to the fascination of channel activity for the players. *Like them, I had incessantly practiced seeing fragmented images as wholes. Time spent in the channels is time striving to see good gestalts*, looking past the interruptions (strategy #5, Figure 4).

Sequences of Images of Similar Form

In a group situation, formal characteristics of entire *sequences* of images may contribute to the sense of closure (strategy #6, Figure 4). Consider when two or more players deploy the same file. In Figure 19, first example, <DuKeCuPiD> and <Charmin^> have played the same script file, creating patterned repetition of the recipient's nick and freshly typed text. ‹DuKeCuPiD› expresses pleasure ("awww we're the same!"). Sometimes even three players manage to play the same file. In the second example in Figure 19, the script changes the order of the colors each time it is displayed on one's computer. It is chance that each activation produced a different sequence of colors.

This phenomenon of enjoying the interactive display of the same or similar files resembles some types of collecting, especially stamp collecting. As when a stamp collector completes a series in which each stamp is of a different color, yet all share a similar design, the individual variations in these images "rhyme" with one another visually (Danet and Katriel 1989). But whereas stamp collecting is ordinarily a solo pursuit, this phenomenon is *interactive*.

Bilateral Symmetry in Image Sets

Image Design and Social Structure

In a study of hooked rugs in a Newfoundland community Gerald Pocius (1979) found that geometric designs containing bilateral symmetry predominated in kitchens, the site of warm chats among friends, whereas asymmetrical figurative designs were disproportionately found in seldom-used parlors, used to host high-status guests. This study suggested that among *rainbow* players too, bilateral symmetry may be an important visual metaphor for egalitarian social

relations and warm feelings of solidarity.

Every year but one since its founding on May 3, 1997 through 2002, *rainbow* celebrated its anniversary with a special show of images created for that occasion (Figure 20).[26] Both upper examples in Figure 20 are perfectly symmetrical. The lower left example is largely symmetrical, but somewhat marred by its central element. The lower right example is asymmetrical. A total of 141 images from four different anniversary celebrations were available for analysis.

As for individual birthday images, I worked with two types, a large "Hallmark"-like set of birthday greetings called "mrBday. mrc"[27] for general use, and three sets of custom-designed images celebrating a specific individual's birthday. The general set contained 161 images by forty-two different artists. As of Summer 2002, there had been three scheduled birthday parties honoring individuals—two for ‹texxy›, a male Texan and the original leader of *rainbow*, in 1998 (thirty-one images) and 1999 (sixteen images), and one for ‹sher^›, in 2000 (fifteen images), a total of sixty-two custom-designed images, by various artists.

Four images in honor of ‹texxy› are shown in Figure 21. The first and fourth are perfectly symmetrical. Large symmetrical objects—a birthday cake and a heart—are placed squarely in the middle of the image. In contrast, the trumpet and map of Texas are highly irregular in shape.

Table 1 compares anniversary and birthday images. While there is some fluctuation among the four

Figure 20

Images celebrating *rainbow* anniversaries. Upper images by <sher^>; lower left by <angltooch>; lower right by <dholli>; balloon and rainbow designs originally by Joan Stark.

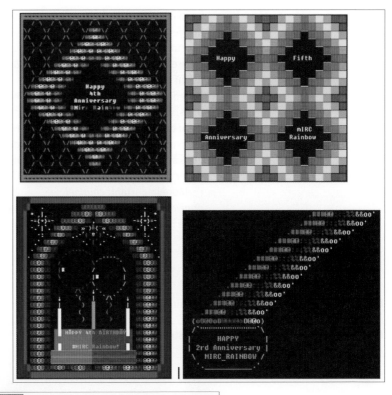

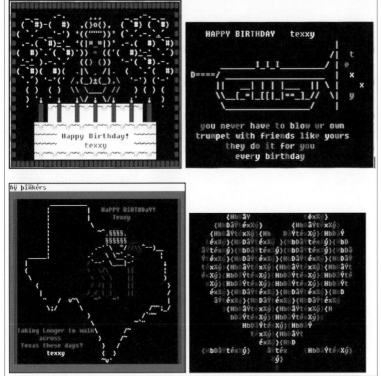

Figure 21

Images in honor of <texxy>'s birthday. Upper row: left image by <sher^>; right image by <glint>, trumpet by Joan Stark; lower row: left image by <Pink_Unicorn>, map originally by <DAV>, man by Joan Stark; right image a script by <texxy> as played by <patches>.

anniversaries, symmetrical images are generally more common than asymmetrical ones (38% vs. 26%). Whereas symmetrical ones are about as common in the general birthday set as in anniversary ones, asymmetrical ones are a good deal more common than in anniversary images (44% vs. only 26% of anniversary images), as expected.[28]

More important, *channel anniversary images are more than twice as likely to be symmetrical*[29] *as individual birthday* images (38% vs. 16%), *and individual birthday images are almost twice as likely to be irregular or asymmetrical.*

Note also an image that ‹texxy› had designed to thank the others at his 1999 online birthday party (Figure 22). From the viewpoint of *gestalt* theory, a square is the next most satisfying shape to the circle. Unlike the circle with its infinite axes of symmetry, the square has four. In addition to vertical and horizontal mirror symmetry,

Table 1 Vertical bilateral symmetry in channel anniversary and individual birthday images (%)

Type of image set	Symmetrical	Somewhat symmetrical	Asymmetrical	Total
1st anniv. 1998	33	33	33	99% (27)
2nd anniv. 1999	41	50	9	100% (22)
4th anniv. 2001	28	40	33	101% (40)
5th anniv. 2002	46	31	23	100% (52)
All annivs.	**38**	**37**	**26**	**100% (141)**
Gen. birthday set	**35**	**21**	**44**	**100% (161)**
‹texxy›'s 1st birthday party	19	23	58	100% (31)
‹texxy›'s 2nd birthday party	19	50	31	100% (16)
‹sher›'s birthday party	7	47	47	101% (15)
All ind. birthdays	**16**	**35**	**48**	**99% (62)**

Figure 22
<texxy>'s thank you to the group at his 1999 online birthday party.

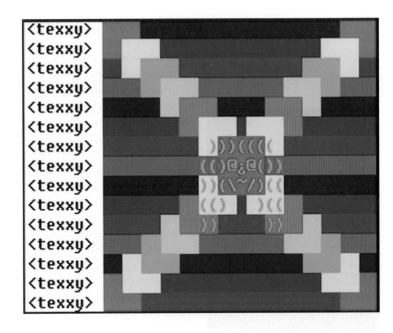

we have two additional diagonal axes. Notice also the smaller, "overlapping" colored squares in each of the four portions of the image.[30] The arrangement of colors is identical in all four sections. Beneath the image, not shown here, was "the line, "I luv mirc_rainbow." It is almost as if he had designed this image with my research questions in mind!

Do the Players Really Care about Good *Gestalts*?

How do we know that the players really cared about good *gestalts*? Were they just having fun with typography and the computer keyboard? Strong indirect evidence can be inferred from interviews: it turns out that the most admired artists were all exclusively or predominantly concerned with pattern and symmetry in abstract designs.

Keeping Artists' Nicks Invisible or Subordinated

But there is also important direct evidence. On August 1 2002, I sent the ops Yahoo list the following question:

Hi gang!

... I've been wondering why most artists think it's OK to put their nick in the offline coding of an image, instead of making it part of the image. This way, the nick doesn't show when the file is played, and people may never know who created it and who deserves credit for it.

Also, when you take a design by Joan Stark ... from the Web and rework it, why is it OK just to put their initials into the code, so they are invisible when the file is played?

Why not add a couple of lines to the file, and have the nick of the artist (and of the ASCII artist too if art by them has been used) visible when the file is played? Couldn't this be part of the border, for instance?

Is there a reason why you don't do this?

I had two research questions in mind. First, for some time I had been trying to understand the players' attitudes toward intellectual property issues. I was puzzled that artists often embedded their nick in the coding of an image, making it invisible when the file was played in the channel; similarly, they credited ASCII artists whose work they had adapted by hiding their initials in the coding.[31] A rare exception was <tera>'s practice of adding a white

```
            Sittin on the
          front porch with doremi
          just a swinging
 B                                          B
 B        /```|       .@@@@,          B
 B       |  bb|_     @@@@@@@@,    B (\/)
 B       c      _)  @@`@@@@@@    B   \/
 B(\/)  \ ._|    (_   ?@@@@    B
|B:\/:~:~)  /:~:~: =' @@@@~:~:B
|B:::::::/\\/`\;_::\ (__:::::B
|B:::::| \ '\__/`'\\//  `\)::B
|B:::::|| | '|::/ /    \ \:::B
|B:::::|| ' \:| \_/\_/  | ::B
|Bo:::\ \   '  |:\_\    /:::::Bo
|"Bo:::=\ \===::/`\%%'/`\:::"Bo
|\"Bo~|  \_\ \|     `""`    |:~:\Bo
 \ \"Bo    )))  \          \:::"Bo
  \ \"Bo:        \          \:::"Bo
   \|~~~~|    -||-  nnnnnnnnnn~~~~|
    `~~~~~~|   ||  ~~|  |_|_|  ~~~|
              ||    | |  |_|_|
              | |   | |  |_|_|
              | |    \   ~~~\__/~~\
 jgs        (    \    \     \_,_)`~._)
               `-._)-~._)
```
Artist jgs
Color By Tera

Figure 23
A work by <tera>, original design by
Joan Stark.

space at the bottom of the image, and entering the names or initials in red (Figure 23).

My second goal was to try to elicit explicit evidence of interest in good *gestalts* as a reason for omitting nicks. Four themes emerged. One was that insiders know where to look for the names of artists, making it acceptable to hide them. <puriel>, a senior op and an Illinois housewife, wrote, "Most IRCers KNOW where to look for the credits. Those that are new soon learn." <MistyDawn> wrote, "most anyone who knows about us and our files knows to SCROLL over the art if you want to see who made what or who colored what."[32]

A few said they hide their nick out of modesty. <puriel> wrote, "adding visible credit lines is like bragging to me. Hiden [sic] is fine." <sher^> said, "I do not want to see my nick everytime someone plays one of my files. Seems egotistic to me. If I draw a castle, I wanna see the castle not my nick." <Catniip>, a female divorced insurance agent from Texas, remarked, "I am not nearly the ascii artist that many ppl [people] in RB [rainbow] are... When I do sign my nick in ascii [sic] it is usually a light grey and doesn't really distract from the art." Although modesty is a factor for <Catniip>, her use of a color that does not distract (her word) from the image also hints at concern with good *gestalts*.

The single most mentioned theme was that of pursuing good *gestalts*, though not in these words. <puriel> said, "We just happen to hide all that *so it doesn't take away from the fun of the file*" (italics added). <serina>,

a Californian divorcee, said, "The reason I do it on the inside is *so it does not [sic] mess up the pic"* (italics added). <kiera>, the Canadian housewife, commented:

I hide them [nicks, initials] cause I think it looks better because if you have alot [sic] of clutter it messes up the popup ... ive [sic] always done it mainly by habit but imo [in my opinion] it looks a lot better ... the less clutter the better. (emphasis added)

<redmoon>, a Texas nurse practitioner, wrote, "I usually hide it [her nick] cause *it takes away from the text"* (italics supplied).[33]

<litty>, an Illinois housewife, called to my attention that when images from packaged sets are displayed, the name of the set, often with the artist's name, is displayed beneath them, obviating the need to display the name on the image (Figure 24). Several artists, including <litty>, insert their nick over and over in the hidden code, making it difficult for others to remove their nick.[34] Figure 25, the full, offline version of the image in Figure 24, including "watermarks" and color codes, shows how much work it would be to remove all traces of the artist's nick. Thus, many artists claim credit for their work in this unconventional manner, while avoiding "messing up the popup." These examples and verbalizations indicate a seventh strategy to pursue closure: when creating images, *to avoid making visible extraneous material that could spoil a good gestalt.*

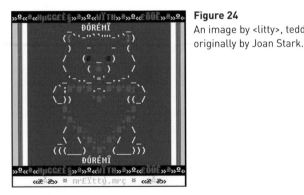

Figure 24
An image by <litty>, teddy bear
originally by Joan Stark.

Figure 25
Offline coding in an image by <litty>,
including "watermarks" and color
codes.

```
/say  ¤11,1»¤15°¤11«¤13ª¤11«¤4HµGG£E§¤11»¤13ª¤11»¤15°¤11«¤4WÏTH»¤11»¤13ª¤11»¤11°«¤4£ÔÔĒ¤11»¤13ª¤11»¤15°¤11«
/say  ¤11,11ï¤13,13u¤15,15m¤5,5ĵudïmlïb¤_ $rbfancy2($upper(%nn)) _¤5,5dablonde¤15,15d¤13,13í¤11,11F
/say  ¤11,11ï¤13,13u¤15,15a¤5,5ĵudïmlïo¤(¤13(¤0`´-^`´"""-'_¤13)¤0)¤5,5dablonde¤15,15d¤13,13í¤11,11¤
/say  ¤11,11ï¤13,13u¤15,15d¤5,5dablonde¤0)       -    (¤5,5dablonde¤15,15d¤13,13í¤11,11R
/say  ¤11,11ï¤13,13u¤15,15e¤5,5ĵudïmlïo¤/     (¤2¤ ¤8_ ¤2¤¤¤)    \¤5,5ĵudïmlï¤15,15d¤13,13í¤11,11M
/say  ¤11,11ï¤13,13u¤15,15b¤5,5ĵudïmlïo¤\    ( ¤4¤  ¤0)      /¤5,5lïbbylï¤15,15d¤13,13í¤11,11Y
/say  ¤11,11ï¤13,13u¤15,15y¤5,5lïbby^¤0  _'-.._'¤8=¤0'_..-'_¤5,5dablonde¤15,15d¤13,13í¤11,11F
/say  ¤11,11ï¤13,13u¤15,15Ɔ¤5,5ĵudïm¤0/`;¤4#'¤4#'¤4#¤0.-.¤4#'¤4#'¤4#;¤0 \¤5,5ĵudïm¤15,15d¤13,13í¤11,11R
/say  ¤11,11ï¤13,13u¤15,15U¤5,5ĵudïm¤0\_))     ¤4,5'#'    ¤0((_/¤5,5ĵudïm¤15,15d¤13,13í¤11,11I
/say  ¤11,11ï¤13,13u¤15,15Ɔ¤5,5lïbbylï¤4,5#.           .#¤5,5lïbbylï¤15,15d¤13,13í¤11,11E
/say  ¤11,11ï¤13,13u¤15,15I¤5,5lïbbylï¤0'#.          .#'¤5,5ĵudïmlï¤15,15d¤13,13í¤11,11N
/say  ¤11,11ï¤13,13u¤15,15M¤5,5ĵudïm¤0/ ¤4'#.       .#'¤0\¤5,5lïbby^¤15,15d¤13,13í¤11,11D
/say  ¤11,11ï¤13,13u¤15,15L¤5,5lïbby^¤0_\  \¤4'#. .#'¤0Ɔ,5/ /_¤5,5ĵudïm¤15,15d¤13,13í¤11,11S
/say  ¤11,11ï¤13,13u¤15,15I¤5,5ĵudïm¤0(((___) ¤4'#'  ¤0(___)))¤5,5ĵudïm¤15,15d¤13,13í¤11,11S
/say  ¤11,11ï¤13,13u¤15,15B¤5,5´10150100   $rbfancy2($upper(%nn))      ¤5,5ĵgs¤15,15d¤13,13í¤11,11S
/say  ¤11,1»¤15°¤11«¤13ª¤11«¤4HµGG£E§¤11»¤13ª¤11»¤15°¤11«¤4WÏTH»¤11»¤13ª¤11»¤11°«¤4£ÔÔĒ¤11»¤13ª¤11»¤15°¤11«
/say      ¤2«¤12æ¤11Á¤12æ¤2» ¤13¤¤14 mr£ïttý.mrç ¤13¤ ¤2«¤12æ¤11Á¤12æ¤2»
```

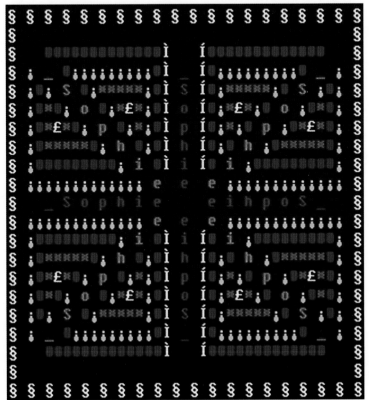

Figure 26
A rare multistable design by
<[blue-]>. Reprinted from
Danet (2001), Plate 6.9.

Figure 27
A design by <sher^> to celebrate
rainbow's fifth anniversary.

Avoiding Multistable Designs

Early in this article I noted that complex good *gestalts* are exceedingly rare in *rainbow* art. A multistable image is one that can be read in more than one way (Ihde 1979: 66–79; cited in Cohen 2000: 102). The image in Figure 26 is the most complex, most multistable one I have documented. The artist, ‹[blue-]›, was active in both *rainbow* and its parent channel *#mirc_colors*. The image was captured just once on *colors*; I never encountered it on *rainbow*, though other art by ‹[blue-]› displayed on *rainbow* is in my corpus.

There are many ways of reading this image. One can focus on the X-shaped black cross, with the nick embedded in it. One can focus on the +-oriented vertical/horizontal cross, or hold the combination of the +-shaped X and the diagonal X together in one's eye. One can focus on the purple letters of the nick. One can see the four blue squares as dominant, or focus on eight blue triangles, arranged in symmetrical pairs. The eye can play with axes of symmetry, "folding" over the vertical, horizontal or diagonal halves of the image. Although this image may be read in many different ways, we experience it as a good *gestalt* because it is highly organized. *Rainbow* artists rarely make viewers work this hard to grasp their images. Even when there is elaborate play with pattern and symmetry, images are generally *unistable*.

An exception to this generalization is interlace designs, which hover ambiguously between two- and three-dimensionality, but are unambiguous in representing metaphorically the interlocked friendships in the group (formed behind the scenes, in private chats, e-mail and phone calls; Figures 14, 27). In short, an eighth strategy to pursue closure is *to avoid creating images which are multistable, even if they are complex good gestalts.*

A Ninth Strategy: Portrayals at a Distance

A final strategy to pursue good *gestalts* is to portray people and animals *at a distance*. Close-ups entirely filling the space (Figure 28) are almost nonexistent in *rainbow* art. In the IRC adaptation of this ASCII image, the head almost bursts out of the frame. Almost always, artists choose and adapt ASCII portrayals of people and animals somewhat from afar, as in Figures 16, 23, and 24.[35]

Discussion

I have argued that the development of pattern and symmetry in this art is profoundly connected to the shift from solo ASCII art to a group-based art, and that, therefore, "closure" and "enclosure" are empirically and not merely etymologically related. Clearly, many forms of repetition in *rainbow* images serve as metaphors for togetherness. One could almost reduce this thesis to a formula:

   "(Visual) twoness = (social) togetherness"

Artists and players pursue an "aesthetic of near-repetition" (Kawin 1972), for the psychological pleasure this gives, and because it expresses visually the players'

Figure 28
An ASCII tiger adapted for IRC by
<sam^>, ASCII artist unknown.

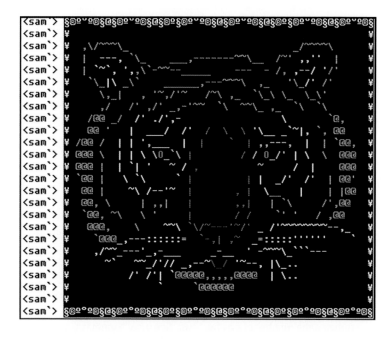

longing for *communitas* (Turner 1969, 1977), for security, love, and acceptance in an insecure, fragmented world (Bauman 2001).

Another indication that this art is inherently social in nature is the fact that *rainbow* artists do not relate to their creations as autonomous aesthetic objects outside the IRC context. I asked artists if they ever printed and hung their art on a wall, or used it in some way other than to communicate online. <sher^> had printed two of her favorite castle series, and hung them on a wall for a while.[36] But she commented, "They seem to lose their depth in printed form," indicating that they looked less impressive when printed, and that she had no interest in doing this again. Even <angltooch>, unusually, a professional artist with an MFA and one of the most senior ops, had never printed any of her IRC

images, though she had printed some computer art she had created with Photoshop. "No," she said, "I enjoy the art in the way it was intended to be viewed, as on IRC." <puriel>, the Illinois housewife, bluntly commented: "Heck no, IRC is just that, IRC … the art is … just for IRC." When she abruptly withdrew from *rainbow* in anger over a demotion in her status as op, she erased all her art from her computer's hard disk.

<puriel>'s dramatic response demonstrates that the art expresses the players' desire for community, but cannot guarantee it. Behind-the-scenes aspects of *rainbow* as a contingent social world, most notably, the elaborate organizational hierarchy that has developed to manage channel affairs,[37] sometimes conflict with its egalitarian goal of togetherness, just as happens in the physical world.

Notes

1. This article extends an earlier presentation of this phenomenon (Danet 2003). On the history of ASCII art and earlier research on IRC art, see Danet (2001), Chapters 5 and 6. Chapter 6 is also available at http://atar.mscc.huji.ac.il/~msdanet/cyberpl@y/.

2. ASCII stands for American Standard Code for Information Interchange. ASCII art is created with the ninety-five typographic symbols that are used in plain text online, e.g. in e-mail.

3. The nicks (nicknames) of all players are presented in angle brackets, just as they appear on IRC.

4. *Rainbow* was created in May 1997, when a group of dissatisfied players on #*mirc_colors* defected to start a new channel. While other channels have been involved with IRC

art, *rainbow* is the best known and the most successful. The IRC software requires that the # symbol precede all channel names. For direct experience of communication on *rainbow*, download and install the Windows program, mIRC, from http://www.mirc.co.uk, activate it, log on, and type */join #mirc_rainbow*.

5. This response rate is nearly 50%. The proportion of committed ops responding is probably even higher; an update of the ops list on the channel website (http://www.mirc-rainbow.net) soon after the interviews were collected reduced the number of ops by a third.

6. The others saw that she had joined them when her nick was added to the list of players present, at the right of the channel window.

7. Unlike ASCII art, this art cannot be printed or viewed offline. See Danet (2003).

8. The players use a Windows 95+-based shareware program called "mIRC" by Khaled Mardam Bey (URL in Note 4), adapted from a plain-text IRC program by Jarkko Oikarinen. The sixteen colors available in Windows may be used.

9. These typographic characters require eight, not seven, bits to encode them.

10. See Arnheim (1954); Koffka (1935); Kohler (1929); Kreitler and Kreitler (1972), Chapter 4.

11. This is a revised version of Danet (2001), Figure 6.5, p. 259. See also my previous research on closure in collecting (Danet and Katriel 1989).

12. One exception is the use of a repeated typographic symbol to create a border around an e-mail signature file.

13. Credits: ‹nightrose›, ‹happyone›, ‹sher^›, and others.

14. See Boas (1955 [1927]); Hatcher (1974); Washburn and Crowe (1988, 2004). The appeal of symmetry is not universal. Japanese traditional culture shows a marked preference for asymmetry and irregularity, see Barthes (1982); Keene (1995).

15. See also Gell (1992, 1996, 1998); von Gwinner (1988); Welters (1999).

16. See also "Symmetry and the Shape of Space," http://comp.uark.edu/~cgstraus/symmetry.unit/; "Symmetry and Pattern: the Art of Oriental Carpets," http://mathforum.org/geometry/rugs/; "The Geometry Center: Symmetric Tilings," http://www.scienceu.com/geometry/articles/tiling/symmetry.html; "An Introduction to Symmetry," http://www.geom.umn.edu/~demo5337/s97a/.

17. See also Stevens (1984); Hargittai and Hargittai (1994); Washburn and Crowe (1988); and the website given in Figure 7.

18. Source: http://www.geom.umn.edu/~demo5337/s97a/students.html.

19. See Kopp and Kopp (1995); for further discussion of hooked rugs, see the section on "Image Design and Social Structure" below.

20. See Danet (2003), Figure 4, for an unusually elaborate

example of heraldic symmetry in *rainbow* art.

21. See the discussion of "Framing and Filling" above, and Dublin (2000); Peesch (1982); Trilling (2001: 135–145).

22. See also Mladenovic (1999) on the protective functions of fringes in Macedonian dress.

23. This predilection for interlace designs seems to conflict with my hypothesis about good *gestalts*, which should not be ambiguous. Interlace images both offer protection from harm *and* visually realize the interlocking of "arms," among *rainbow* friends. Simple good *gestalts* are far more prevalent than complex, multistable ones such as interlace designs. See Figure 27 and its accompanying discussion below.

24. The Christmas wreath also appears in *rainbow* art.

25. "Queen Anne de Bretagne at Confession," page from a prayer book by Jean Poyet for Anne de Bretagne. Tours, France, *ca*. 1492–5, the Pierpont Morgan Library (Poyet *ca*. 1492–5).

26. The 2000 show was merely a reshowing of earlier art, and was therefore omitted from the analysis. No anniversary celebration took place in 2003.

27. This is an abbreviation for a "mirc_rainbow birthday" collection. "mrc" denotes a set of images for use within "mIRC."

28. Since complete sets of images are being compared, no statistical tests are needed.

29. I am referring only to bilateral vertical symmetry, not to other types discussed in this article.
30. Only the central component is not a true square.
31. In earlier years they had not bothered to do even this, but did so increasingly, in response to criticism from ASCII artists.
32. That is, moving the cursor over the image while holding down the space bar reveals the hidden nicks and initials.
33. She means "text art," not verbal text.
34. Unusually, this artist uses four different nicks.
35. Also, the thematic content of typical figurative images suggests a preference for images that make people feel good—angels (Figure 11), teddy bears and hearts (Figure 24), and other cute animals (Figure 16). Images that domesticate potentially harmful forces (the cute devil in Figure 5) are far more common than those enhancing their potential for harm or aggression (Figure 28).
36. There *are* technical obstacles: in order to print an IRC image, it must first be converted to a regular graphic image.
37. Remarkably, since 2003 and perhaps even earlier, the group distinguishes eight ranks for ops, with the highest rank going to the leader, or, in IRC parlance, channel "owner." See http://www.mirc-rainbow.net/rbops.html.

References

Amir, Ziva. 1977. *Arabesque: Decorative Needlework from the Holy Land*. New York: Van Nostrand Reinhold.

Arnheim, Rudolf. 1954. *Art and Visual Perception: A Psychology of the Creative Eye*. Berkeley, CA: University of California Press.

——. 1982. *The Power of the Center*. Berkeley, CA: University of California Press.

Barthes, Roland. 1982. *Empire of Signs*. New York: Hill and Wang.

Bauman, Zygmunt. 2001. *Community: Seeking Safety in an Insecure World*. Oxford: Polity Press.

Boas, Franz. 1955 [1927]. *Primitive Art*. New York: Dover.

Cohen, Erik. 2000. *The Commercialized Crafts of Thailand: Hill Tribes and Lowland Villages* (Collected Articles). Richmond, Surrey: Curzon.

Danet, Brenda. 2001. *Cyberpl@y: Communicating Online*. Oxford: Berg Publishers. Companion website: http://atar.mscc.huji.ac.il/~msdanet/cyberpl@y/.

——. 2003. "Pixel Patchwork: 'Quilting in Time' Online." *Textile: The Journal of Cloth & Culture* 1: 118–43.

Danet, Brenda and Tamar Katriel. 1989. "No Two Alike: Play and Aesthetics in Collecting." *Play and Culture* 2: 253–77.

Dublin, Trinity College Library. 2000. "The Book of Kells." CD-ROM. Trinity College Library Dublin.

Fordham, Frieda. 1953. *An Introduction to Jung's Psychology*. Baltimore, MD: Penguin.

Gell, Alfred. 1992. "The Technology of Enchantment and the Enchantment of Technology." In J. Coote and A. Shelton (eds) *Anthropology, Art and Aesthetics*, pp. 40–67. Oxford: Clarendon.

——. 1996. "Vogel's Net: Traps as Artworks and Artworks as Traps." *Journal of Material Culture* 1: 18–31.

——. 1998. *Art and Agency: An Anthropological Theory*. Oxford: Clarendon.

Gombrich, Ernst. 1984. *The Sense of Order: A Study in the Psychology of Decorative Art*. London: Phaidon.

Grabar, Oleg. 1992. *The Mediation of Ornament*. Princeton, NJ: Princeton University Press.

Hargittai, Istvan and Magdolna Hargittai. 1994. *Symmetry: A Unifying Concept*. Bolinas, CA: Shelter Publications.

Hatcher, Evelyn Payne. 1974. *Visual Metaphors: A Formal Analysis of Navajo Art*. St Paul, Minnesota: West.

Hildburgh, Walter Leo. 1944–5. "Indeterminability and Confusion as Apotropaic Element in Italy and in Spain." *Folklore* 56: 134–49.

Ihde, D. 1979. *Experimental Phenomenology*. New York: Putnam & Sons.

Jackson, Anna. 1997. *Japanese Country Textiles*. London: Victoria and Albert Museum.

Kawin, Bruce F. 1972. *Telling It Again and Again: Repetition in Literature and Film*. Ithaca, NY and London: Cornell University Press.

Keene, Donald. 1995. "Japanese Aesthetics." In Nancy G. Hume (ed.)

Japanese Aesthetics and Culture: A Reader, pp. 27–42. Albany, NY: State University of New York Press.

Koffka, K. 1935. *Principles of Gestalt Psychology*. New York: Harcourt Brace.

Kohler, W. 1929. *Gestalt Psychology*. New York: Liveright.

Kopp, Joel and Kate Kopp. 1995. *American Hooked and Sewn Rugs: Folk Art Underfoot*. Albuquerque, NM: University of New Mexico Press.

Kreitler, Hans and Shulamith Kreitler. 1972. *Psychology of the Arts*. Durham, NC: Duke University Press.

Liungman, Carl G. 1991. *Dictionary of Symbols*. New York: WW Norton.

Mladenovic, Vesna. 1999. "Threads of Life: Red Fringes in Macedonian Dress." In Linda Welters (ed.) *Folk Dress in Europe and Anatolia: Beliefs about Protection and Fertility*, pp. 91–110. Oxford: Berg.

Ortega y Gasset, José. 1986. "Meditations on the Frame." In Richard Brettell and Steven Starling (eds) *The Art of the Edge: European Frames, 1300–1900*, pp. 21–5. Chicago, IL: Art Institute of Chicago.

Paine, Sheila. 1990. *Embroidered Textiles: Traditional Patterns from Five Continents*. London: Thames & Hudson.

Peesch, Reinhard. 1982. *The Ornament in European Folk Art*. New York: Alpine Fine Arts.

Phillips, Peter, and Gillian Bunce. 1993. *Repeat Patterns: A Manual for Designers, Artists and Architects*. London: Thames & Hudson.

Pocius, Gerald L. 1979. "Hooked Rugs in Newfoundland: The Representation of Social Structure in Design." *Journal of American Folklore* 92: 273–84.

Poyet, Jean. *ca.* 1492–5. "Prayer Book of Anne de Bretagne." Tours, France. *Pierpont Morgan Library*.

Purdon, Nicholas. 1996. *Carpet and Textile Patterns*. London: Lawrence King.

Riegl, Alois. 1992 [1893]. *Problems of Style: Foundations for a History of Ornament*. Princeton, NJ: Princeton University Press.

Schapiro, Meyer. 1994. "On Some Problems in the Semiotics of Visual Art: Field and Vehicle in Image-Signs." In Meyer Schapiro (ed.) *Theory and Philosophy of Art: Style, Artist, and Society*, pp. 1–32. New York: George Braziller.

Stevens, Peter S. 1984. *Handbook of Regular Patterns: An Introduction to Symmetry in Two Dimensions*. Cambridge, MA: MIT Press.

Traber, Christine. 1995. "In Perfect Harmony? Escaping the Frame in the Early 20th Century." In Eva Mendgen (ed.) *In Perfect Harmony: Picture and Frame 1850–1920*, pp. 222–47. Seattle, WA: University of Washington Press.

Trilling, James. 2001. *The Language of Ornament*. London: Thames & Hudson.

Turner, Victor. 1969. *The Ritual Process: Structure and Anti-Structure*. Chicago, IL: Aldine.

——. 1977. "Frame, Flow, and Reflection: Ritual and Drama as Public Liminality." In Michel Benamou and Charles Caramello (eds) *Performance in Postmodern Culture*, pp. 33–58. Milwaukee, WI: Center for Twentieth Century Studies, University of Wisconsin.

von Gwinner, Schnuppe. 1988. *The History of the Patchwork Quilt: Origins, Traditions and Symbols of a Textile Art*. West Chester, PA: Schiffer.

Washburn, Dorothy K. and Donald W. Crowe. 1988. *Symmetries of Culture: Theory and Practice of Plane Pattern Analysis*. Seattle, WA and London: University of Washington Press.

—— (eds). 2004. *Symmetry Comes of Age*. Seattle, WA: University of Washington Press.

Welters, Linda (ed.). 1999. *Folk Dress in Europe and Anatolia: Beliefs about Protection and Fertility*. Oxford: Berg.

Weyl, Hermann. 1952. *Symmetry*. Princeton, NJ: Princeton University Press.

Wilson, Eva. 1994. *Ornament, 8,000 Years: An Illustrated Handbook of Motifs*. London: Thames & Hudson.

Digital Imagination: The Impact of Digital Imaging on Printed Textiles

Abstract

Digital imaging technology is providing textile practitioners with a medium that is changing and challenging the processes used in the generation and production of printed textile artifacts. The phenomenological research being undertaken at University of Wales Institute Cardiff indicates that when the technology is used as a creative medium rather than a production tool it facilitates an evolving visual language, new hybrid craft practices, and the opportunity for collaboration through the sharing of digital imagination. The findings reveal that since physical experience in the world informs thought and fires imagination, future developments in computer interfaces and humanization technology will provide even greater opportunities for the creative exploitation of the media by printed textile practitioners.

A number of innovatory printed textile artists and designers based in the USA and Europe who are using digital imaging in their creative practice have contributed to this research through informal interviews, personal correspondence, and case studies.

CATHY TREADAWAY

Cathy Treadaway is the Research Assistant (Textiles) at the University of Wales Institute Cardiff, UK and is currently investigating the impact of digital imaging on printed textile practice for a PhD research project.

Trained as a surface pattern and textile designer she has worked digitally since 1982 and has been an exponent of computer-aided surface pattern and textile design within UK art education since the early 1980s. She has worked as a surface pattern and textile designer for industry worldwide for the last sixteen years and has exhibited regularly internationally.

Textile, Volume 2, Issue 3, pp. 256–273
Reprints available directly from the Publishers.
Photocopying permitted by licence only.
© 2004 Berg. Printed in the United Kingdom.

Digital Imagination: The Impact of Digital Imaging on Printed Textiles

The use of digital imaging by contemporary printed textile practitioners is revealing changes not only in the artifacts produced but also in the approaches taken to generate concepts and imagery. The development of visual ideas in the abstract dimension[1] of virtual space provides opportunities for artists to explore, innovate, and craft in a medium that can be shared and communicated in new ways (McCullough 1996). The phenomenological research being undertaken at University of Wales Institute Cardiff indicates that the practice of artists and designers of printed textiles is being challenged by the use of digital imaging technology as a medium that extends the imagination into a new arena. The evidence gained as a result of field and case study interviews reveals how computers are providing a rich medium through which complex images can be developed, collaboration between practitioners is facilitated, and new methods for physical crafting and elaboration are being provoked.

Kay argued in 1984 that the computer is "not a tool though it can act like many tools" but rather a metamedium possible of conjuring "media that cannot exist physically... with degrees of freedom for representation and expression never before encountered" (Kay 1984). Others who are aware of the potential of the technology have affirmed this view and Briggs (1997), Bunce (1994), Harris (1999), and Leak [(1998)] have noted the technology's potential as a metamedium in the design and simulation of textiles. The blurring of the boundaries between production tool and metamedium in the domain of printed textile design is resulting in changes in working processes, development of new hybrid craft techniques, and a changing visual language of pattern and color on cloth. The evidence for this is revealed in the practice of those who are not constrained by the economic concerns of industry, in the work of artists and academics who have time to explore and reflect upon the processes that they employ.

The development of computer-aided design (CAD) technology in the printed textile industry has been largely driven by its use as a production tool (Leak 1998). Its implementation for innovation of design concepts has been less rapid than its adoption for the reworking of hand-rendered artwork for colorways, repeats, and for prototyping fabric samples. Even in companies such as Liz Claiborne who have pioneered the introduction of the electronic design studio, digital innovation continues to be supplemented by hand-rendered paper or fabric artwork that is scanned and manipulated electronically. There is not always a temporal advantage in working in this way as it can often take as long to render artwork electronically as by hand, but the opportunity to alter colors, scale, and repeat is greatly enhanced once the design exists in the virtual domain (Crawford 2000) (Figure 1). It also facilitates the communication of design visualization between designers within the company and to suppliers and retailers, providing opportunity for intervention in the design process prior to manufacture. Crawford refers to this as "design by committee" (Crawford 2003). The visual impact of these changes on commercially manufactured printed textiles is less evident than the reduction in product development cycle time and economic benefit accrued. This, however, is likely to change as the developments in digital ink-jet printing provide systems that meet industrial production speeds and become economically viable.

Textile design practice has always been linked with production methods and tools. Each technological change has impacted on the visual outcome of the textile produced (Bunce 1994)

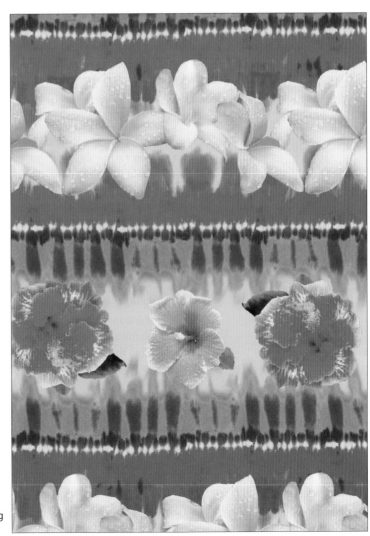

Figure 1
Debra Bernath—Floral stripe, commercial digitally printed design for children's swimwear incorporating scanned and photographic imagery.

and the technical skills required to use the technology have inevitably created a distance between the designer and the product; the original artwork being interpreted and adapted to the meet the requirements of production. Bunce argues that the use of digital imaging software and ink-jet fabric printing is providing an opportunity for this trend to be reversed:

By removing the intervening stage of engraving, jet printing can create closer relationships between the designer CAD, and the textile product. This may impact upon design processes and also change what designs are for and how they are seen. (Bunce 1999)

The integration of digital processes, particularly digital ink-jet printing technology, is changing the visual characteristics produced and stimulating a renewed interest in physical interaction with the cloth. The digital tool is becoming a medium for digital imagining.

A Changing Language

Briggs and Bunce contend that the legacy of technological progress in the production of printed textiles has been the adoption of stylistic change into the designer's visual vocabulary.[2] Each change creates "a visual language that contains a wide range of dialects and which expands as new developments occur" (Briggs 1995). Briggs argues that the use of photography and digital imaging in the design of printed textiles is producing a "new visual language" (Briggs 1997). The technology is providing opportunities for practitioners

to explore images in new ways, for example through micro detail or combined layered image, extending the artists' aesthetic experience and knowledge. This is being communicated through the characteristics of expressed visual language within the domain: in the nature of the imagery used, the complexity of image produced, and the vocabulary of color.

Digital ink-jet printing has eliminated the need for repetition in a textile design since the traditional constraints of roller printing no longer apply.[3] It is proposed that this new-found freedom should inspire the use and generation of new complex pattern forms (Bunce 1994). Bunce argues that CAD has the potential for providing new types of repeating pattern:

Computer image manipulation capabilities provide fast, accurate and flexible methods of pattern construction... In this way CAD could be used to create new types of design with non-mechanized appearances. (Bunce 1994)

This new approach to the construction of pattern can be seen in the work of Hilary Carlisle, who is exploring the use of computer-aided randomization techniques to apply variations to small-scale motifs. The digitally printed fabric outcome has the initial appearance of repeated image but with "continual visual variety" (Bunce 2003). Hele Abild, a Danish designer, has taken a similar approach. Her digital textiles appear to contain repeating elements but in fact they change

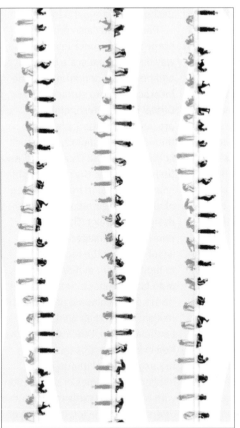

Figure 2
Hitoshi Ujiie—
Falling, ink-jet
digitally printed
fabric.

Figure 3
Hitoshi Ujiie—Everybody,
ink-jet digitally printed
fabric.

Figure 4
Hitoshi Ujiie—Flowers, installation of
digitally printed fabrics, *Technology as
a Catalyst: Textiles at the Cutting Edge*,
The Textile Museum, Washington, DC.

subtly across the surface of the cloth (Campbell 2003). The uses of repeat and non-repeat are explored in the work of textile artist Hitoshi Ujiie. In his textile piece "Falling" (Figure 2) he is able to convey the rhythm of repeat through non-repeating image and at the same time explore the concept of movement through image and motif. The textile "Everybody" (Figure 3), which makes use of letterforms, dismisses the notion of both repeat structure and conventional textile motif. Ujiie was one of the six contemporary artists who use digital printing or weaving to create their art, who exhibited work in the *Technology as a Catalyst: Textile Artists at the Cutting Edge* exhibition at the Washington Textile Museum in 2002. His digitally printed installation textile pieces contained single large-scale motifs based on computer manipulated photographic imagery of natural forms. They contain no elements of repeat but are rhythmic in their arrangement within the installation (Figure 4).

Photographic imagery has been integrated into surface pattern and textile designs for the last decade as a result of four-color process and heat transfer printing (Briggs 1997). The potential of digital cameras to capture images has inspired a number of designers whose main concern is exploiting photography to create textile design imagery. Briggs' research at Nottingham Trent University explored the potential of photography in relation to digitally printed cloth, questioning the applicability of such complex visual images in the structure of a textile

design (Briggs 1997; Bunce 2003).

Photography also provides scope for an exploration into the way distance and scale is perceived and how focus and format can be incorporated into surface design. Digital imaging technology is providing opportunity for these themes to be explored, as evident in the work of J. R. Campbell at Iowa State University. His photographic imagery is used in the production of digitally engineered garment designs (Figure 5). The use of photographic imagery on textile is not new[4] but the recent ability to digitally print millions of colors onto fabric is inspiring artists and designers to combine photographic realism within their work. The textile art of the Dutch artist Wilma Kuil exemplifies this through her use of digital photographic imagery, sometimes in conjunction with traditional textile motifs and often through the intermingling of virtual and physical layers of motif.

Digital photography and video is providing a rich source of visual data that can be utilized to inspire and to create design imagery. Rebecca Earley, Senior Research Fellow at Chelsea College of Art, for example, has described the role of the computer in the development of her visual concepts as "a massive scrapbook, a massive sketchbook" (Earley 2003). Working with a digital camera and scanner she is able to make use of collected visual data from a variety of sources and blend them into one in the electronic dimension. A similar blending of visual data is evident in the work of the American textile artist Susan Brandeis who uses both a physical sketchbook and photographic

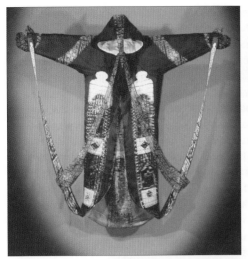

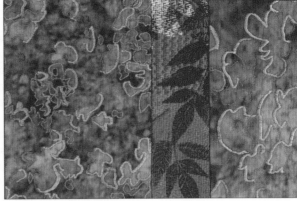

Figure 6
Susan Brandeis—Quintessence, detail, digitally printed, mixed media fabric construction.

Figure 5
J. R. Campbell—Cathedral, digitally engineered ink-jet printed garment.

Figure 7
Susan Brandeis—Messages from the Past, digital print, dye, felted, reverse appliqué, embroidery.

Figure 8
Alison Bell—Berneray Bird, ink-jet digitally printed silk.

imagery scanned and manipulated digitally to amalgamate a variety of images from a specific geographic location to convey her sensuous response to that particular place. Her aim is to produce an image that gives the viewer multiple simultaneous glimpses of the original location comparable with the way the eye informs the mind, as it perceives a place in time. The image is digitally printed and then embroidered to provide additional layers of meaning and narrative. The computer facilitates a "more literal image" of her chosen visual environment (Brandeis 2003). It is evident that the use of visual imagery of such complexity could only be considered as a direct result of access to digital printing technology (Figures 6 and 7).

It is this complexity and detail made possible through the use of digital imaging and ink-jet digital printing technology that has became the inspiration for a new body of work for the textile artist Alison Bell. She uses layering to build and manipulate imagery that is photographic, hand-rendered, and electronically generated to form a complexity of image that could not have been achieved any other way. Bell describes the use of digital imaging as a "totally new visual language" that is "full of words that I didn't know existed" (Bell 2003) (Figure 8). A wealth of detail and use of layered imagery has featured in the textile art of Joan Truckenbrod since the 1970s. Her work reveals an exploration of superimposed image, both photographic and digital, and her recent installation pieces strive to "produce a richly layered experience for the viewer through

a confluence of numerous media: video projection, digital imagery, fiber and sound" (Ullrich 2003). The ease with which the technology can provide connections between electronic devices is aiding the development of the vibrancy of the visual language evident in her work. The complexity of the images used by Truckenbrod, Brandeis and Bell are indicative of the potential of the emerging visual language to communicate sensuous experience and conceptual depth.

Color

The complexity of image has been made possible as a direct result of the availability of a huge color palette provided by digital printing technology. Unlike analogue printing systems in which the printing of large numbers of colors is economically prohibive, digital ink-jet printing facilitates the use of thousands in any one printed image. The level of detail, hue, and tonal range is also massively increased. The impact of an extended gamut and arrangement of colors is described by both Bell and Earley as contributing to the developing visual language. Bell describes it as comprising of new "colours, textures, surfaces, subtleties" (Bell 2003) and Earley states that, "the design work being produced now compared to 1996 is just so radically different ... the use of colour is more ambitious, it's more varied, the amount of texture and detail within one design is much, much broader... The inclusion of so much detail and colour on one piece of fabric is what the language is all about" (Earley 2003).

According to Leak, "The number of colours the human eye can differentiate is unknown. Scholars believe between one and ten million colours can be differentiated" (Leak 1998). Computer monitors, however, are capable of producing up to 16.4 million colors, far more than the human eye can see. This seductive and vast color range available on the monitor inspires practitioners with the desire to achieve the same results as printed product. It fires the imagination in the virtual domain but is also the source of great frustration. The color output from digital printers is frequently disappointing, as their gamut does not match that of the monitor.[5] Color is also changed by the substrate onto which it is printed and the light source by which it is viewed. The issues of color management and communication are having a significant impact within industry, and research is currently under way to overcome these difficulties through the provision of a global digital color communication standard. The aim is to provide accuracy of spectral data that can be used in software, comparable with Microsoft Word in its ubiquity, which will provide a universal language of color. The Society of Dyers and Colourists are carrying out this enormous task in conjunction with the American Textile Chemists and Colorists Committee.

The accuracy of spectral data, however, is not the only concern in the use of virtual digital color. The work of Land, the color scientist and inventor of the Polaroid camera, revealed that the appearance of a color depends on its context, not just the wavelengths reflected from the sample. He proved that all colors perceived in a scene supply the brain with information about a given object that is used to reinterpret this data (Leak 1998). Our perceptions are also shaped by our experiences (Merleau-Ponty and James 1964). Sight alone is not vision, but what we perceive is molded, changed, and adapted by the brain (McCullough 1996). Color is therefore dependent on perception and interpretation. For the digital practitioner, the interpretation of additive primary (light) color information from the computer monitor simultaneously with that of subtractive primary (pigment) color of printed product is an additional difficulty.

Leak argues that there are currently two ways of approaching the problems of using digital color.

Designers using systems, soon realise that there are restrictions in terms of colour and, therefore, they work with and around them, dependent on the specific working context. When a CAD system is treated as a medium, these restrictions become characteristics of the system. From this perspective poor colour fidelity may not necessarily be so problematic. Indeed what are termed colour mistakes, when looking at a CAD system as a production tool, can be seen as catalysts for change if they are approached from a different perspective. (Leak 1998)

Alison Bell embraces this heuristic approach to the disparity of printed color. When she encounters a color problem she will "work with it" and use the lack of fidelity in the printed outcome to stimulate further her creative process. This is achieved by combining the printed image with a hand-rendered silk painting technique to create a new expression of the original concept.

New Craft Techniques

The assumption that ever-improving technology replaces craft (Dormer 1997) can be challenged by a number of the textile artists interviewed for the research who are incorporating digital technology within their process and evolving new hybrid craft techniques. For some of these practitioners the frustration with the cloth outcome as a result of digital printing has led to a new inquiry into surface ornamentation; for others the technology itself has inspired development of a particular craft. The lack of hands-on crafting in physical space is regarded by some as being detrimental to the printed textile outcome. Many of those interviewed have commented on the digitally printed cloth as being flat[6] and lifeless due to both the effect of color and the lack of physical intervention in the process. Brandeis writes:

To work with these kinds of fabrics we will have to find ways to re-establish a relationship with the materials, to reclaim the images from the machine, and to convert the monologue of the machine printed product to a dialogue between artist and cloth. (Brandeis 2003)

For Brandeis this dialogue is reestablished through the embellishment of the textile surface by a variety of textile crafting techniques. She refers to the need for embellishment of the digitally printed surface that is "more gestural and expressive, in order to keep the surface rich and tactile" (Brandeis 2003). Her experience of hands-on crafting of textiles has provided her with a depth of tacit knowledge that motivates her desire to intervene physically in the textile surface. Investing time and craft skill in the digital print to enhance it with the qualities that contribute to a textile's "visual and emotional power" (Brandeis 2003).

In his essay "The Work of Art in the Age of Mechanical Reproduction" (1934), Walter Benjamin uses the term "aura" to describe the emotive element that is lacking in the machine-manufactured product. The aura of a crafted product is a unique accumulation of responses to a material and is derived from the hands-on workmanship of risk involved in human manufacture (Pye 1964). For Brandeis, Bell, and Earley the printed digital image lacks aura. It demands further hands-on intervention and elaboration. Initially Bell found the digitally printed product to be inhibiting; "I was transfixed by the quality and it stopped me looking beyond it." She describes it as being too "perfect" (Bell 2003). Earley describes digitally printed cloth as being "too flat" and having "no sensual product quality about it," and regards it as being "a stage in between" rather than a finished product. She advocates further

manipulation of the fabric surface involving over-printing, laser cutting or the design of a product or garment utilizing the printed cloth. Each elaboration involves the introduction of the element of risk; the textile might be damaged or even destroyed in the process. The physical intervention, however, also provides "material evidence of tool usage. Something about its authorship and origins" (McCullough 1996). The textile artifact becomes no longer the product of the machine but a crafted expression of the artist's imagination.

The ease with which it is possible to create a digitally printed fabric and the freedom with which it is possible to incorporate diverse and personal imagery has encouraged practitioners to incorporate them within their work as an expressive means of communicating their narrative. The artist Michael James now uses his own digitally generated and printed imagery, rather than artisan-produced fabrics, to apply imagery that is more personal and appropriate to the pieces. The detail that he can include is changing the visual outcome of his work. This is exemplified in a piece created in 2002 called "A Strange Riddle" (Figure 9). James makes use of digital imaging technology to combine images from childhood memory with concepts that are personal and universal, assembling, layering, and manipulating them to communicate his theme. The digitally printed imagery is constructed and embellished with machine embroidery and quilting detail and provides continuity and

Figure 9
Michael James—A Strange Riddle,
ink-jet digitally printed and quilted
fabric.

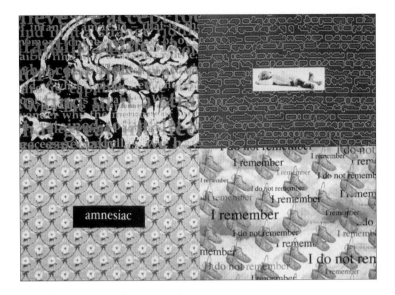

Figure 10
Michael James—The Nature of Truth,
ink-jet digitally printed and quilted
fabric.

Figure 11
Amy C. Clarke—Tell Tale Apple,
beaded textile with detail.

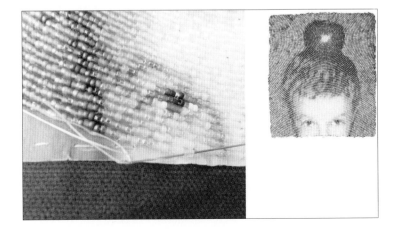

depth to the expression of the narrative (Figure 10). This is similar to the approach taken by the bead artist Amy C. Clarke. Her narrative is generated through digitally manipulated photographic imagery to explore story telling, myth, and legend. The themes are narrated both through the imagery used and the ancient Native American spiral-embroidered craft technique she employs. The image to be beaded is photographed, scanned, and manipulated in Photoshop®. Once digitally printed, the image is applied to fabric and the beads are applied by hand stitching. The choice and positioning of the beads relates to the light-reflecting qualities of the digital pixelation on the computer screen (Figure 11). The impact of the technology on the practice of both these artists has contributed to the development of the narrative content of their work.

The use of digital imaging as a medium to layer photographic, scanned, electronically generated imagery and color in the virtual domain provides opportunities for the artist to imagine and explore concepts, narrative, and visual arrangements without commitment or expense. Images can be amended, constructed, and deconstructed providing multiple explorations and iterations in much the same way as imaginary thought is explored in the mind. The digital media captures the visual product in a virtual space, a semi-reality, making it possible to be communicated back to the artist for reflection and to other artists and designers providing a means for creative collaborative intervention.

Collaboration

The textile designer J. R. Campbell explores this collaborative potential in his "art to wear" developed with the fashion designer Jean Parsons. Their work involves the integration of textile design into garment shape to produce bespoke printed garments (Campbell *et al.* 2002). A recent project included collaboration of a third designer, Susan Strawn, whose contribution of a knitted section to the garment used the printed imagery created by Campbell in the garment pattern designed by Parsons (Strawn 2003) (Figure 12). The Campbell and Parsons collaboration built on previous research at North Carolina State University and by designers at [TC]2, the Textile Technology Corporation, investigating the use of photographic imagery with complex garment pattern forms, striving to overcome the difficulties associated with the alignment of odd-shaped pattern pieces, darts seams, and their disruption of the surface pattern of the print. The Campbell–Parsons collaboration is continuing in current research exploring the possibilities of creating bespoke customized children's wear marketed and sold entirely through the Internet.

The possibilities of bespoke or customized products is also being researched by Philip Delamore at the London School of Fashion who is concerned with the application of three-dimensional printing of garments using rapid prototyping technology. His collaboration is a scientific one and reveals a new type of digital imagining possible through a three-dimensional modeling process.[7] It is also

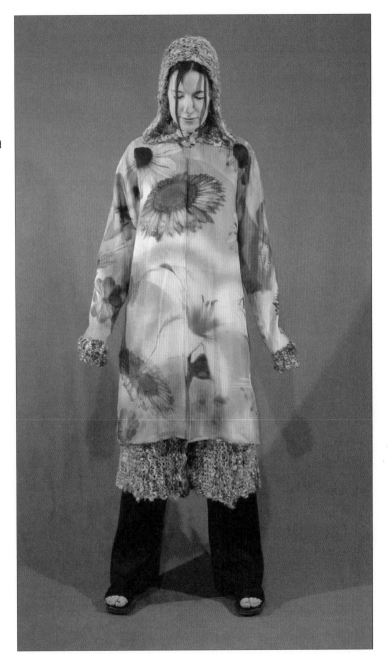

Figure 12
J. R. Campbell, Jean Parsons,
Susan Strawn—Summer, engineered
garment collaboration.

evident that the Internet and
e-mail is providing a new arena for
collaborative design innovation.
A recent collaborative research
project involved Elaine Polvinen,
a textile designer from New York

State, USA, Shen Li a designer
from Beijing, China, and Yimee
Wang from Taiwan. The aim of
the project was to "use email to
develop a collaborative digital
design culminating with a Chinese-

inspired theme exhibition"
(Polvinen 2003) and involved the
communication of imagery via a
private website and e-mail as tiny
thumbnail images. The digital
media provided the platform for the

meeting of minds, sharing of visual information, and development of concepts as well as existing as a tool for communication.

Imagining in a Make-believe World

Imagination is defined as the *image forming power of the mind* or the *power of the mind that forms conceptions* (English Dictionary). Its role is that of visualizing in a domain outside the physical world in order to "create" a new idea, description or artifact (Collingwood 1958). The virtual world of cyberspace could be said to provide an extension to the image-forming power of the mind, providing a further means for the development and visualization of concepts. The virtual world is, however, the product of the imagining of others; *make-believe* is central to the conception and design of software (Laural 2001). Design software provides the user with the make-believe world of the utopian studio in which airbrush and oil paints can blend onto the same paper surface. The symbolic and iconic language perpetuates the metaphor. The breadth of scope provided by the virtual studio contains so much embedded knowledge and skill that it has been described as being "knowledge beyond replication" (Gale 1994) since its sum is greater than that possible for any individual to acquire. There are however hidden dangers in this domain. There is the possibility of being enframed in the software engineers' logic (Marshall 1999) and of being seduced by the visual effects of particular functions and techniques rather than the pursuit of creative exploitation to achieve the artist's aesthetic objective (Braddock and O'Mahony 1998).

For many textile practitioners the greatest difficulty lies in their ability to enter into this world. Access is gained through an understanding of the programmers' logic and the interpretation of symbols. It requires acquisition of tacit skills to provide the freedom to interact with the embedded knowledge and tools intuitively so that the imaginative power is released to form the image. This requires time for practice and exploration and in a temporally challenged society this is may create difficulties due to the complexity of software applications. As a result, some artists prefer to limit themselves to certain functions of the software so that fluency in these techniques provides opportunity for creative thought.

The implicit logic of the digital medium does not lend itself to the spontaneity many artists crave in the generation of their work. Through experimentation and familiarity with software functions, however, it is possible to engineer a form of unpredictability. Alison Bell has developed a fluid working process that provides her with a form of spontaneity she regards as essential to her practice. Using scanned hand-painted silk fabric samples and multiple layering, Bell is able to intervene in the image using digital painting and erasing functions. Her layers are built from line work that is input into the computer using a tablet and pen, collected images in scanned photographic form, and electronic images from the Internet. The use of the virtual space for layering of images enables her to capture and trap memories that form her expressive response to the environment her textile art reflects. The images are digitally printed on to silk and often over-painted and sometimes elaborated with stitch and appliqué. They are inspired in the digital domain and developed through the interaction of materials and hand crafting techniques (Figure 13).

Imagine the Future

Software has been described as a "collaboration between the imaginations of the creators of a program and the people who use it" (Trend 2001). It is the potential of the virtual space to be entered and shared for the communal imagining that is so intriguing. As the imaginative and computational power of the virtual world expands so do the possibilities for digital imagining. Immersive reality is providing opportunities to enter

the image space and interact and intervene creatively with it in real time (Grau 2003). The development of haptic sensors and research into the humanization of technology being carried out at Media Lab MIT (Seelig 2003) may provide new types of interface that will ultimately provide greater accessibility for textile practitioners to enter into the digital virtual domain.

Today's commonly used design hardware systems are not geared to the normal working practice of artists and designers, and interfaces such as mice and keyboards feel alien and unresponsive. For many practitioners sketching with a pencil and paper is one of the fundamental ways of generating ideas; it is a means of making thought visible and exploring the abstract concepts held in the imagination prior to their physical development. If the computer interface is complex, slow, and restrictive the creative flow may be inhibited or even halted. The

research work being carried out as part of the Tacitus project at Edinburgh University is using haptic sensors to explore the issues surrounding development of interfaces that "would enable idea formulation and creative activities to be performed with the same intuitive and fluid transmodal interaction as sketching on paper" (Shillito 2002).

The phenomenological premise is that experience has a questioning character and that our physical approach to the world shapes how it appears to us. Merleau-Ponty contends that consciousness, thought, and memory unfolds "from our condition as being physically immersed in the world" (Cazeaux 2000). The ability of practitioners to touch, sense, and craft their ideas in the virtual world is likely to provide an even deeper stirring of the digital imagination. The effects of this on the printed textile outcome must remain for now conjecture, a figment of our own imagination.

Figure 13
Alison Bell—Cuneiform, digital image.

Notes

1. Malcolm McCullough describes how computers make abstract thought visible: "Concepts become things. We can't touch them yet, but already we can look at them, point at them and work on them as though with hand held tools" (McCullough 1996: 81).
2. An example of this is the way in which floral designs have dominated printed textile designs since the importation of Indian prints in the seventeenth century. The emulation of techniques and stylistic influence resulted in the European "Indienne" designs that were subtly adapted visually to suit a European market. Prior to this floral motifs did not predominate.
3. The repeat of an image or pattern on cloth was historically necessitated by the circumference of the roller (the drop) and its width, which determined the size of the unit of repeat.
4. Amanda Briggs (1997) details this in her PhD thesis.
5. Leak (1998) writes: "Printers create colour by subtractive optical mixing, the majority using a mixture of cyan, yellow and magenta inks ... The printer is unable to reproduce all the colours that the average human eye can see. While some colours are common to both devices, there are printer colours not covered by the monitor and vice versa."
6. Brandeis comments: "The digital prints looked more like paper than cloth. They seem flat, literal and not tactile" (Brandeis 2003).
7. See http//:www. freedomofcreation.com.

References

Bell, A. 2003. Interview with the author. Isle of Arran.

Braddock, S. E. and M. O'Mahony. 1998. *Techno Textiles: Revolutionary Fabrics for Fashion and Design*. London: Thames & Hudson.

Brandeis, S. 2003. *Post-digital Textiles: Re-discovering the Hand*. "Hands On" Surface Design Conference, Kansas.

Briggs, A. and Bunce, G. E. 1995. "Breaking the Rules: Innovatory Uses of CAD in Printed Textiles." *Ars Textrina* 24: 185–203.

Briggs, A. 1997. "A Study of Photographic Images, Processes and Computer Aided Textile Design." PhD thesis, Nottingham Trent University, Nottingham.

Bunce, G. E. 1994. "The Effects of Technological Developments on Pattern Structures used in Printed Textiles." *Ars Textrina* 22: 129–62.

Bunce, G. 1999. *CAD and the Role of the Printed Textile Design*. CADE 99, University of Teesside, CADE.

Bunce, G. 2003. *The Impact of Digital Printing on Textile Design Research*. Denmark: Designskolen Kolding.

Campbell, J. R. 2003. "Digital Wanderers." fiberscene.com accessed 2003.

Campbell, J. R., Jean Parsons and M. Stieglitz 2002. "Digital Apparel Design Process: Placing a New Technology into a Framework for the Creative Design Process." *Design Research Society* 2003.

Cazeaux, C. 2000. *The Continental Aesthetics Reader*. London, Routledge.

Collingwood, R. G. 1958. *The Principles of Art*. London: Oxford University Press.

Crawford, C. 2000. "Liz Claiborne CAD: The Possibilities Are Endless." *Executive Technology*.

Crawford, C. 2003. Lecture to Surface Design Conference. Kansas.

Dormer, P. 1997. *The Culture of Craft: Status and Future*. Manchester: Manchester University Press.

Earley, R. 2003. Interview with the author. Chelsea College of Art, London.

Gale, C. 1994. *Modelling Creative Practice*. Birmingham: Birmingham University.

Grau, O. 2003. *Virtual Art*. Cambridge, MA: MIT Press.

Harris, J. 1999. *Preparing a Medium for The Next Millennium: The "Crafting" of Computer Graphics: A*

Textile Makers Perspective. Design Cultures 1999, Sheffield Hallam University.

Kay, A. 1984. "Computer Software." *Scientific American* 25(3): 52–9.

Laural, B. 2001. "Computers as Theatre." In D. Trend (ed.) *Reading Digital Culture*, pp. 00–00. Malden, MA and Oxford: Blackwell Publishers.

Leak, A. 1998. *A Practical Investigation of Colour and CAD in Printed Textile Design*. Nottingham: Nottingham Trent University.

Marshall, J. 1999. *The Role and Significance of CAD/CAM Technologies in Craft and Designer Maker Practice; With a Focus on Architectural Ceramics*. Cardiff: University of Wales Institute Cardiff.

McCullough, M. 1996. *Abstracting Craft: The Practiced Digital Hand*. Cambridge, MA and London: MIT Press.

Merleau-Ponty, M. and James, M. Edie 1964. *The Primacy of Perception, and Other Essays on*

Phenomenological Psychology, the Philosophy of Art, History and Politics. Edited, with an introduction, by James M. Edie. Evanston, IL: Northwestern University Press.

Polvinen, E. 2003. "West Meets East: Collaborating across Continents." *Surface Design Journal* 28(1): 16–21.

Pye, D. W. 1964. *The Nature of Design*. London: Studio Vista.

Seelig, W. 2003. "Digital Dialogues: Technology and the Hand." *Surface Design Journal* 28(1): 6–11.

Shillito, A. M. 2002. The Tacitus Project. Pixel Raiders.

Strawn, S. 2003. "Expanding the Digital Edges." *Surface Design Journal* 28(1): 12–15.

Trend, D. 2001. *Reading Digital Culture*. Malden, MA and Oxford: Blackwell Publishers.

Ullrich, P. 2003. "Materialized Resonance: The Work of Joan Truckenbrod." *Surface Design Journal* 28(1): 23–7.

Textile Patterns and Their Epistemological Functions

Abstract

Textile work can be interpreted as physical evidence of human thought and actions. Generally artifacts are examined and interpreted as a material expression of culture. This article offers another way of looking at textile patterns, focusing on their production processes. Consequently, textile techniques need to be described in order to demonstrate the constitutional skills of textile patterns. The analysis of textile pattern is, according to this thesis, not undertaken within a style or design history or as part of theories on ornament. A techno-morphological description reflects on spatial conditions and production techniques.

The formulated definition of the term "pattern" introduces the ideas of rhythm, symmetry, repetition, and dimension. These keywords lead to further reflections on patterns of more general interest. Research in different disciplines, predominantly in the natural sciences, deals with all kind of patterns. Cognitive sciences state that pattern matching and pattern construction are required means of complexity reduction, a key function of human behavior. The prerequisites for pattern recognition, the significance of patterns, and its cultural implications within scientific theory are usually not discussed. Here, pattern analysis is proposed as an analytical tool in the search for subjective influences, e.g. in scientific display. Formulating the epistemological function of patterns may benefit interdisciplinary research and support the interface between cultural and natural sciences.

KERSTIN KRAFT

Kerstin Kraft is the first graduate "textile scientist" in Germany. She has worked on various exhibition projects and currently teaches cultural history of textiles at Dortmund University. Her main subjects in research are basic textile phenomena like folding, cutting and patterning.

Textile, Volume 2, Issue 3, pp. 274–289
Reprints available directly from the Publishers.
Photocopying permitted by licence only.
© 2004 Berg. Printed in the United Kingdom.

Textile Patterns and Their Epistemological Functions

Introduction: Patterns Attract Perception

Patterns of behavior, genealogical patterns, patterned design, grid patterns, fan patterns, patterns of growth, Islamic patterns, pattern books, mosaic patterns, Paisley patterns, weave patterns, coat patterns … we live in a universe of patterns, as the American mathematician Ian Stewart puts it (Stewart 1998: 11).

Being attracted by different kinds of patterns, analogies in material, design, history, etc., I started to think about connections and similarities. Looking for a "pattern theory," I only found theories on ornament, as well as descriptions and classification systems of two-dimensional patterns (Gombrich 1984; Riegl 1923; Wilson 1996). The research took shape during this period of collecting patterns and ideas about patterns, organized by the word and the phenomenon "pattern." The analysis of patterns of all dimensions leads to elementary human skills and questions of scientific theory, cognition, and communication. Humans and their systems can be viewed as pattern-searchers.[1] A model is required to link this abstract level to concrete patterns, whether in nature or in art. Models in scientific theory serve to visualize thinking. Taking textile patterns as a model with a focus on their production techniques, we have in addition a utilitarian approach. Textile work provides physical evidence of human thought and action; not only fashionable, beautiful, superficial objects far removed from the world of scientific research.

This article has three main strands. The first is to develop another perspective from which textile patterns can be viewed, allowing us to postulate the significance of patterns in creating textiles. The second is to introduce the textile model as an index of the scientific importance of studying textile creation. Finally, we will discuss the meaning of patterns in the process of knowledge acquisition.

Methodological process will not be discussed in this article. For this cross-disciplinary approach a method had to be developed and refers mainly to Jacques Derrida and characteristic qualities of constructivism.[2]

The basis of reflection is my definition of the term "pattern." Through this definition, the ideas of rhythm, repetition, symmetry and dimension are introduced. Thereafter, the textile model is explained and exemplified by two textile techniques: knitting and plaiting. Looking towards natural sciences and medicine we review their use of patterns and then move to a conclusion with regard to the epistemological function of patterns.

Definition: Patterning the Patterns

A pattern consists of regularly repeated units, a unit being the smallest unique example. Repetition is possible in all dimensions and is potentially infinite. A unit can be a repeat, a motif, a design, a device, a numerical order, a succession of tones or steps. These units often serve as means of classification, e.g. pomegranate pattern or a *pas de chat* in ballet.

Pattern recognition is a process of isolation and abstraction: one needs to recognize the individual units and the construction of the pattern, the rule of repetition. Patterns are the result of repetitions in time and space. They prove connections between motion and form and by this the experience of time and space. Repetition is the main characteristic feature of the pattern and the condition of its infinity. The rule of repetition defines the dimensionality and position of the units. Symmetry and rhythm as systems are able to describe these time and space relations. The textile model is evidence that patterns have more than two dimensions: beyond the three dimensions of the textile object there are further dimensions. Barber for example refers to the messenger function of textile patterns: "Patterned cloth in particular is infinitely variable and, like language, can encode arbitrarily any message whatever" (Barber 1994: 149).

Symmetry and Beauty in Scientific Theory

In mathematical terms symmetry is a process of transformation, a working concept. Depending on the transformation, the motions, and their direction, there are reflection, translation, rotation and glide reflection forms of symmetry. Following that thesis, the maximum of symmetry is the fictitious state of rest.[3] But human perception and patterns of nature are not as perfect as mathematical ideals. For that reason the term "rhythm" is appropriate to describe the repetition not of the same but something very similar. By this patterns are included that are not perfectly symmetrical but are nevertheless recognized as a pattern by the human eye.[4]

The definition given includes all patterns, both material and immaterial, the pattern as design, as model, as patron, as process, as artifact. This is a key step in the perception of patterns as more than visual objects. But there is a remarkable tendency to visualize patterns, to make them visible by their notation.

Introducing the terms of symmetry, rhythm, and repetition helps to establish a scientific approach to patterns, especially in mathematics. During the last twenty years mathematics has become a science of pattern that is concerned with the description and mathematical representation of patterns and their logical and computational understanding. The mathematician Keith Devlin defines mathematics as the science of abstract patterns that are the essence of thinking, communication, calculation, society, and simply life (Devlin 1998: 9). This understanding of mathematics orientated on a phenomenon like pattern provides the opportunity for cross-disciplinary research: patterns can connect cultural and natural sciences. Until now exchange has been reduced to patterned artifacts to illustrate and visualize methods of natural sciences, to describe "symmetries of culture" (Washburn and Crowe 1988). The latter is a reductive but very stimulating approach. An interesting example for natural scientific illustration is a textile model used by the Hungarian chemist István Hargittai. He argues "that analogies from outside crystallography greatly facilitate the understanding of this concept" (Hargittai 1984: 1033). He chooses Hungarian folk needlework in order to explain the one- and two-dimensional space-group symmetries. There are 230 three-dimensional space-groups of crystals, but "unfortunately no needlework analogies," as Hargittai noted (Hargittai 1985: 35). This is a further example of the perception of patterns as a two-dimensional phenomenon. Real needlework, a textile object, has three dimensions, the notational form Hargittai has chosen, does not (Figures 1 and 2).

This connection reveals another quality of patterns: their beauty attracts the scientist. The question of whether aesthetic properties of theories are a sign of truth are discussed by several authors (Mainzer 1988; McAllister 1996): Theoretically, symmetry and simplicity serve as indicators. Using this definition of pattern, including symmetry and a quasi-natural human attraction to the beauty of patterns, pattern research can contribute to scientific theory research. Using the textile analysis as a model, I will show that pattern recognition

Figure 1
The seven one-dimensional space-
group symmetries illustrated by
Hungarian folk needlework. Top
to bottom: translation axis, glide-
reflection plane, translation on
rotation, translation by transverse
symmetry planes, translation
axis combined with a longitudinal
symmetry plane, combination of a
glide-reflection plane with transverse
symmetry planes, and combination
of translation axis with transverse
and longitudinal symmetry planes.
Courtesy of István Hargittai and
Wiley-VCH, Weinheim.

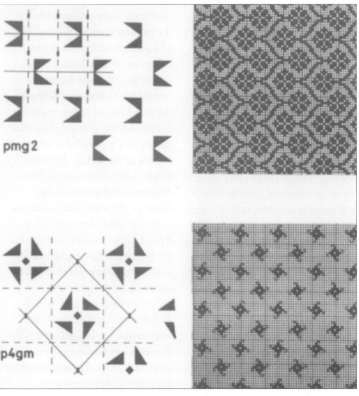

Figure 2
Two examples of the seventeen two-dimensional space-
group symmetries in Hungarian needlework. pmg2,
pillow-slip decoration with scrolling stern motif; p4gm,
blouse-arm embroidery. Courtesy of István Hargittai and
Wiley-VCH, Weinheim.

does not necessarily mean the
assumption of truth, but of sense.
This means that patterns are
important in order to obtain and
to produce knowledge. How this
is done is discussed in the second
part.

For the moment it is important
to separate these two levels
as follows: on the one hand,
to see the textile analysis that
actively follows the pattern as
an epistemological figure; on
the other, the pattern serves as
an analytical tool for scientific
theory research. Patterns need
to be recognized in scientific
work in order to define their
mostly unintentional, passive
instrumentality. On both
levels the definition is still the
same, including and using for
interpretation the qualities of
symmetry, repetition, rhythm, and
dimension.

Textile Pattern Analysis
Textile patterns are usually
treated within a style or design
history or as a special kind of
ornament. Neglecting materiality
of ornament and patterns they

become abstracta and flat pure form (Irmscher 1984). The term pattern is then commonly connected with a two-dimensional form of decoration. Art history usually defines ornament as "der Schönheit additiv angestücktes Beiwerk"—additionally joined accessories (Kroll 1987: 7). This implies patterns fulfill a secondary role, or indeed, none.

I will undertake an analysis of textile pattern that focuses on the production processes and environment in order to show that patterns *do* have functions. The textile production model provides material evidence of pattern-producing processes referring to manual intelligence.

A techno-morphological description of two examples—knitting and plaiting—serves to question textile techniques with respect to the significance of patterns.[5] The main difference to standard methods (for classification or iconographic interpretation) is to *start* from the technique, the process and not the product. The descriptions address spatial conditions, reviewing hand movements and gestures innate to the production process. Textile genesis is itself pattern.

Knitting
The Seiler-Baldinger systematization defines knitting as "mesh formation with a continuous element of unlimited length." The use of a tool, the needle, refers to a higher level of technical development and defines it as a "technically advanced primary method" (Seiler-Baldinger 1994: 23). "In knitting, the loops are arranged in a horizontal row (not

interloped) and connected to the corresponding meshes of the preceding row" (Seiler-Baldinger 1994: 24). The stitch is the binding element of single-threaded textiles.

When we apply the pattern definition to knitting, the motif or unit is the stitch and the rule of repetition derives from the knitting process. The operation to link the stitches is an active and rhythmic action with a direction of motion that creates symmetries on different levels. The potential infinity of knitting patterns refers to the unlimited thread length.

The technique of knitting considered as pattern construction reveals some basic elements. Historically round knitting precedes flat knitting (Rutt 1987: 23). In order to "invent" flat knitting one has to imagine the operation from the other side or, one has to perform a symmetrical reflection operation. This operation produces two different types of stitches, called "plain and purl." In German—translated literally—you have right and left stitches and the "wrong side" is called the "left side" as well.

During the knitting process the needle permanently pierces the piece of work from the front to the back. In flat knitting this experience from two different sides is even more pronounced by turning the piece of work at the end of each row. Knitting with both hands, which is not common, would avoid this turning and instead produce a reversal. The working direction depends on the handedness: a right-handed person knits from right to left (most left-handed persons do the same because they are taught to conform

when introduced to the technique of knitting).

If plain and purl stitches change within a row (producing patterns like ribbed knitting or basket knitting) the work acquires plasticity; a further effect is stability: the balance of power prevents the edges from rolling up. The order of stitches in a row, and the connection of the stitches in the vertical, build up a system of coordinates. In terms of differential calculus the operation of decreasing and increasing at the edges produces a diagonal with a gradient (Figure 3).

The experience of infinity is apparent when knitting. Rutts' "temporary definition" of knitting makes this clear: work is reversible, until the yarn is cut. But even after casting off one can start the working process at the edges (e.g. when knitting socks) or from the plain fabric (e.g. to knit a pocket) and thus dimensional experience is created. This and other liberties in technique and design to be found in knitting cause the lack of a knitting notation. In contrast, the weaving system within its binary system of weft and warp allows strong formalization and mechanization resulting in a dominance of woven cloth.

This dominance is not only to be found in fabric production but also in the interpretation of textiles as texts, focusing on their linearity. According to Jacques Derrida, the dominance of linear writing causes logocentrism in metaphysics (Derrida 1983: 128). This implies a Western predominance that is perceptible in textile analogies as well. The technical preconditions

Figure 3
Decreasing at the left edge.

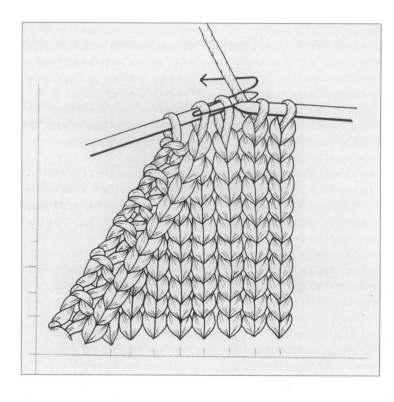

for weaving and felting find parallels in lifestyles. A nomad, a typical example of a felt creator, has a lifestyle pattern determined by the weather and the seasons with some degree of predictability. Weaving requires planning and stability. With the loom or the field as the determinant, the only movement will be a predictable to and fro. Settled people weave and write in linear and geometric forms, living in a system of coordinates. The motion of the shuttle corresponds to the plough. Written languages, which change their direction after every row, are called—with homage to the ox –"boustrophedon-writings." And the ox and the house, symbols of settlement, are the source elements of the alphabet. Typically nomads do not have a written culture, their "houses" are transient in nature and permanence is not a predominant feature of their way of life (Deleuze and Guattari 1992: 554). Greenblatt shows that this fact leads to Euro-centric arrogance equalizing (linear) writing with history and tradition (Greenblatt 1998: 22).

Plaiting, Braiding or Basket Weaving

The German word "Flechten" describes the action of textile working whereas the words plaiting, braiding and basket weaving are connected with a specific material or product. For the following I will use the word "plaiting" which has the most general meaning. The difference to mesh formation is the use of thread systems instead of continuous elements (Seiler-Baldinger 1994: 26). A thread system requires planning and measurement.

With the description of plaiting techniques I will show the importance of textile work examination for research, e.g. within the historiography of mathematics. One section of the historiography of mathematics is ethno-mathematics or ethno-geometry. Paulus Gerdes, one of the main protagonists, describes ethno-mathematics as a cultural anthropology of mathematics and mathematical didacticism (Gerdes 1997: 1). He studied mathematical knowledge of indigenous people in former colonies in order to explore the origins of geometry; uncharted territory when compared to the development of counting and numbers.

As far as source material is concerned, Gerdes had to develop his own method with a focus on operation analysis. For this purpose he chose a textile technique: plaiting. Thus it was that one of the most abstract sciences was explained by a primary human action. Gerdes explains his choice: on the one hand he refers to the ancient history of textile techniques. Herein he agrees with Elizabeth Barber. She supposes that "the textile industry is older than pottery and perhaps even than agriculture and stock-breeding" (Barber 1991: 4). On the other hand, he takes as a hypothesis their knowledge-producing qualities. Gerdes writes

that the regularity of plaited products teaches humans to recognize patterns and to use them afterwards for geometrical forms, art, and mathematical analysis (Gerdes 1990: 109). Applying his method he questions every step of the operation to establish which geometrical idea is important for the next step. By this he looks for rigid geometrical thinking. Through action human beings learn to recognize geometrical forms in nature and in their own production (Gerdes 1990: 272).

I will cite only a few examples of Gerdes' research to demonstrate that textile techniques have contributed to develop human pattern recognition skills, pattern production and, as a result, to formulate abstract knowledge.

Braiding with three elements may be viewed as the origin of plaiting; according to Gerdes it was the answer to the practical need of strong fibers. The regularity and ordered change of over and under is the result of human work and not its natural state. The experience of advantageous regular forms brings to mind the meaning of order (Gerdes 1990: 74). The change of over and under recalls the development of weaving techniques from plaiting. The difference is the angle of the fold appearing at the edges (selvages when weaving). Consequently, the production and comprehension of the 45° and the 90° angles, mathematical basics, are the results of plaiting and weaving. Further, he describes a dialectical reciprocal action between experiment, material qualities, and establishment of purpose when basket weaving. To

create a stable basket with holes you need a repetitive pattern, e.g. with a 60° starting angle at the edges, which produces hexagonal forms. During this activity symmetry is permanently created, unconsciously but as a visible product. According to Gerdes, plaiting led to a kind of pre-comprehension with respect to symmetries. There are other textile techniques like "sprang"—which he does not address—creating symmetry in operation and in the material product in a most obvious manner. The characteristic center line of the sprang technique corresponds with the axis of reflection symmetry.

These short references should be seen and interpreted in the context of the initial questions regarding the significance of the textile model and of patterns. Patterns are textile constituting. The repetition of working units, whether understood as a repeat, or not, generates the textile object. Consequently all textile techniques are based on the idea of patterning: an isolated unit (repeat) is repeated with potential infinity. So we can state: patterns are not accidental but substantive to textiles.

Taking textile working as physical evidence of abstract knowledge, we can assume that the operational aspects of patterns perform ontogenetic functions. The repetitive operation teaches the human to compare. Basic experiences of space and orientation, orthogonal systems, differentiation between interior and exterior, and the relational positioning of the self are obtained.

Epistemological functions may also be deduced. The ability to observe and reproduce patterns helps to comprehend numbers and angle relations, connections from form and plane and form and motion. The geometrical forms and regular qualities of patterns provide evidence of a primary comprehension of order. Working with flexible textile material in one-, two- or three-dimensional forms leads to a basic comprehension of symmetry and infinity. At the same time, the empirical experience leads to an understanding of the necessity of order (symmetry).

From Textile to Scientific Theory

The examination of textile works—creating and viewing them—teaches the comprehension of patterns and related fundamental experiences. Applying this model to a more general view, textile works can be read as material evidence of pattern recognition, pattern matching, and pattern construction in order to provide structure to the world.

Whenever we recognize a pattern we are inclined to assume sense or significance. As a consequence many approaches to patterns try to decode them, try to read patterns like an alphabetical text, searching for a grammar. Gardin's research of ornament codes reached a peak. He takes ornaments, defines signs that constitute these ornaments and creates a syntax with them in order to create a formalized description model. As a result a simple linear pattern is transformed to "+fiximuli KA." He understands this as a

preliminary working basis for objective interpretation by means of mechanization (Gardin 1978: 7, 29). Other authors are more interested in formalization and less focused on interpretation. Wersin for example comprehends patterns and ornaments as "language," a kind of writing preceding the "invention" of the alphabet (Wersin 1953: 25).

My approach is not focused on what patterns show or represent, but assumes that they are able to show *something* and I investigate how they do that. It is perhaps a statement of the obvious, but there is no doubt that humans (and animals) have a particular awareness of patterns. Patterns attract perception; this phenomenon is based on the function of pattern differentiation, an elementary brain process, namely complexity reduction. As such, pattern recognition marks an important element of viable behavior. Most patterns are perceived visually. As we know visual perception is not passive but an active process of construction (Hoffman 2000: 184). Consequently pattern differentiation influences further pattern recognition.

Within scientific theory this is of importance when studying the pattern attractor effect on the scientist. At the beginning of this article I described the effect on me. I have been attracted by patterns of all kinds, especially the ideas of visual analogies and hidden meaning. After a while I recognize this conditioning and start thinking about it. This meant changing the level and search patterns of thought and recognition within scientific work.

I find that the analysis and impact of patterns are cognitive processes in natural sciences, but the cultural impact is not discussed. There are many examples for research initiated by the attractor effect of patterns. Regular patterns in nature arouse scientific curiosity. Regularity as a sign of significance means excluding contingency. A recent example is the huge stone patterns identified in the subarctic zone. Two American scientists found a model to describe the development of these patterns based on self-organization processes (Werner and Kessler 2003).

The biologist Hans Meinhardt was attracted by the beauty of sea-shell patterns, while eating in an Italian restaurant. He states that until now, we have not considered the possible reasons behind these patterns (Meinhardt 1997: VI). His interest focuses on examining complex nonlinear pattern construction taking the sea-shell patterns as a model. These models serve as historical minutes: a seemingly static object bears witness to dynamic natural processes. This is a good example of the meaning of beauty in sciences. The natural beauty attracts the scientist, the beauty of the models, the man-made algorithms, are afterwards taken as a sign of truth (Figures 4–6).

No in-depth consideration is given to this mathematical operation, this translation

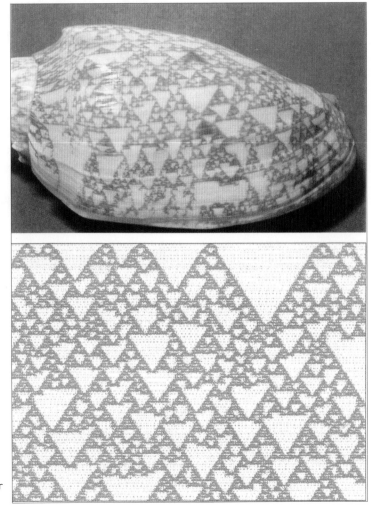

Figure 4
The pattern of *Cymbolia innexa* Reeve resembles the Sierpinsky-Triangle of Fractal Geometry which evokes knitted patterns. Courtesy of Springer Verlag.

Figure 5
Bifurcations in *Oliva porphyria* and the
simulated hormone dissemination.
Courtesy of Springer Verlag.

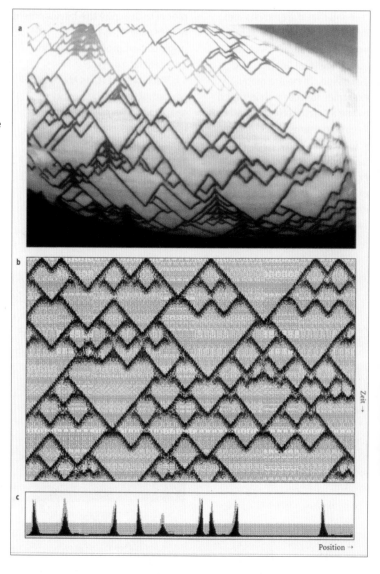

into numbers. One reason for
this credulity is the quality of
patterns of symmetry, rhythm,
and repetition. The recognition,
regularity, and beauty of patterns
are attractor and evidence in the
same time. Ian Stewart reflects
on these issues and states that
symmetry and geometry are human
inventions, whereas mathematics
is required to describe them and
comes forth from the universe
(Stewart and Golubitsky 1993:
278, 285). Douglas Hofstadter
speaks of God as a mathematician.
Does the atheist have any other
alternative to the thesis that
numbers proceed from the Primary
One? And reviewing DNA structures
might lead a textile scientist
to the assumption that God is
familiar with macramé (a knotting
technique producing very similar
spirals).

Figure 6
"Salt and Pepper" (a textile pattern name), here a pattern calculated with mathematical rules of symmetrical tiling. Courtesy of Birkhäuser Verlag.

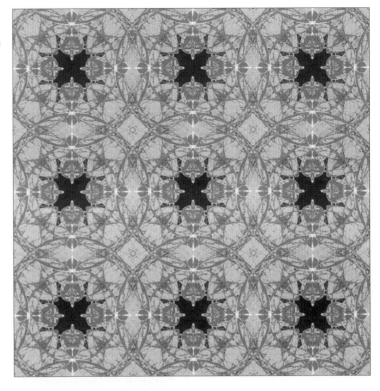

With respect to the following and final examples for the use of patterns within scientific display, the image of a knotting God is exaggerated but not completely absurd. This example is taken from the field of medicine and shows the impact of culture on science (Figures 7 and 8).

In the 1950s a technique enabling production of cardiac images was developed, which is called the M-Mode-Echocardiogram. This technique generates motion curves. The motion of cardiac structures in relation to the transducer is calculated and displayed graphically. These are technical patterns of digital imaging: the sonographic patterns of the

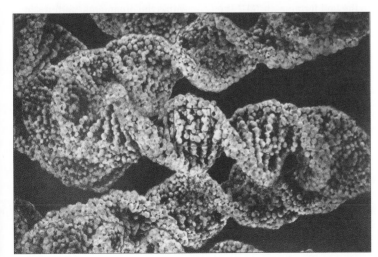

Figure 7
The DNA helix structure.

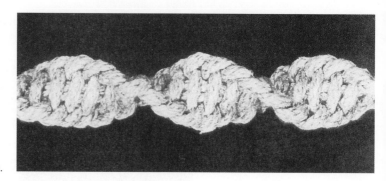

Figure 8
Knotted spiral—macramé technique.

cardiac structure are modeled. Initially a pattern forming the letter "M" was found. This pattern can be described as the attractor of scientific attention. Perception of this pattern gave rise to further observation and research. Proving the argument that patterns imply deeper meaning.

Statistical calculations serve to define the norm and aberrations from it. In this case the "M" was defined as the healthy state. Taking my definition of the term pattern, we can state: a valve cycle consisting of a valve movement of the anterior and the posterior mitral valve leaflet corresponds to the unit forming an "M." The healthy heart repeats this "repeat" forming a glide reflection (rhythm); the potential of which depends on the life span.

The similarity of the curve with the letter "M" and its symmetrical qualities (which were well synchronized with the image of valve movements) led to the statistical work and the establishment of a diagnostic method. Technical progress and the use of reference methods revealed the need to review the definition of the norm. The form is

now an asymmetrical "M," which is only described as "M" in keeping with the tradition.

This example serves to show the constructive nature of diagnostic techniques supported by medical apparatus and its dependency on culture. Prerequisites for the recognition of the "M" are literary and symmetrical awareness.

Going back to the above-mentioned formalized description model of ornaments from Gardin we can now observe this as a doubling process. Unintentionally Gardin demonstrates the use of patterns as cognitive and cultural models. He tried to find the pattern within the ornaments/patterns in order to handle them. He ignores his own subjectivity, his cultural condition, and preferences.

When starting to look for patterns on this level, we will find them everywhere: patterns in language and writing, patterns in art, patterns in movements like sports or dance, patterns in architecture, patterns in music . . . all researched within a scientific community with its own theories and methods.

A simple but key pattern is the binary code of zero and one. The use of the binary code is usually traced back to the invention of the model weaving loom by Joseph-Maria Jacquard in 1805. The pattern to be woven was converted into a code of holes punched in a card. The aim of complete computerization reinforces the search for patterns in order to find the rule of repetition and the translation.

Conclusion: The Epistemological Function of Patterns

We can find patterns everywhere, as micro- and macro-structures, on fabrics as well as on tires and animal coats. Collecting and classifying them is therefore a never-ending process. My intention was not to find a new category or reinterpret specific patterns but to identify the pattern as an epistemological figure.

Pattern recognition and pattern construction are important human skills as a part of basic cognitive equipment. The process of comparison is inspired by the visual attraction of patterns. Comparison leads to ordering and categorization—fundamental problems of cognition. Pattern matching means viable behavior. My research started with the examination of material evidence of this behavior.

The textile analysis serves to change the perspective at different levels. Within textile sciences patterns are marked as textile-constituting processes. Consequently textile patterns are not reduced to attributive function like ornaments. Detailed examination, techno-morphological descriptions, can be applied to all textile patterns or techniques from "simple" spinning to highly complex analysis with patterns on different levels and dimensions. Contextualization of patterns within dress and material culture studies can serve as a starting point when examining a dress as a material or as a represented object, e.g. analyzing the conditions of representation. Pattern analysis should be a part of technical analysis of dress and textiles in order to extend interpretation and to reflect on notation systems, on systematic and description procedures. Besides research on specific patterns, like the pomegranate pattern, patterns can be questioned as a phenomenon. The moiré pattern is a good example to examine on a cross-disciplinary basis in natural sciences as well as in philosophy, art, and material culture (Kraft 2002: 173).

Using textile analysis as a model we can state the primary function of patterns in complexity reduction. Textile working is a trainer for these processes. The obvious constructivity of textile patterns and their notation can be useful to evidence that other patterns are man-made as well. As the various examples above showed, implications of construction of the translation modus must be considered.

Even if one is not a radical proponent of constructivism, one has to admit that instruments of research are developed by humans and are not revealed as being God given. Constructivism demands transparency in the process of knowledge acquisition, by this an analysis of fact-producing processes is required and not a philosophical fact justification. Using patterns as epistemological figures, as demonstrated, serves to examine conditions of knowledge acquisition and knowledge production. Pattern examination can reveal the significance of individual and collective cultural conditions, like gender, socialization, geographical conditions, fashions, etc. for scientific research.

Human beings need patterns as a means of differentiation from perception level to organization of knowledge up to the most abstract forms of thinking about thinking.

Notes

1. The physician and discoverer of the quark, Murray Gell-Mann, describes complex adaptive systems as pattern-searchers (Lewin 1993: 28).

2. Derrida wrote a part of the formation report for the Collège International de Philosophie (Derrida 1990: 551–76). He creates the French terms "Limitrophie" and "intersection transversale" in order to describe scientific processing that ignores disciplinary limits and limiting scientific language. I used the term "Limitrophie" for a linguistic operation and performative action: limitrophical motions define proceeding. Main ideas of constructivism were important for the position of the observer/ the scientist (Maturana 1998: 26). My doctoral work treats the methodological approach and the introduction of a textile model in extension (Kraft 2002).

3. Stewart gives the example of
a motionless lake: each point
of the surface is like the other.
Symmetry breaking produces
patterns: a drop evokes a
pattern of rings (Stewart 1998:
103).
4. The research of symmetry is
a large field and includes the
terms asymmetry, dissymmetry,
antisymmetry, symmetry
breaking, and questions
concerning the constructivity of
symmetry perception (Field and
Golubitsky 1993; Hargittai 1986;
Weyl 1955).
5. The idea and the term refer
to the techno-morphological
researches of the French
paleontologist André Leroi-
Gourhan (mainly Leroi-Gourhan
1971 and 1973).

References
Barber, Elizabeth W. 1991.
Prehistoric Textiles. Princeton, NJ:
Princeton University Press.

Barber, Elizabeth W. 1994.
*Women's Work. The First 20,000
Years*. New York/London: Norton.

Deleuze, Gilles and Félix
Guattari. 1992. *Kapitalismus und
Schizophrenie. Tausend Plateaus*.
Berlin: Merve Verlag.

Derrida, Jacques. 1983.
Grammatologie. Frankfurt am
Main: Suhrkamp.

Derrida, Jacques. 1990. *Du droit à
la philosophie*. Paris.

Devlin, Keith. 1998. *Muster der
Mathematik*. Heidelberg/Berlin:
Spektrum Akademischer Verlag.

Field, Michael and Martin
Golubitsky. 1993. *Chaotische

Symmetrien*. Basel: Birkhäuser
Verlag.

Gardin, Jean-Claude. 1978. *Code
pour l'analyse des ornements*.
Paris: Éditions du Centre National
de la Recherche Scientifique.

Gerdes, Paulus. 1990.
Ethnogeometrie. Bad Salzdetfurth:
Verlag Barbara Franzbecker.

——. 1997. *Ethnomathematik*.
Heidelberg: Spektrum
Akademischer Verlag.

Gombrich, Ernst.1984. *The Sense of
Order. A Study in the Psychology of
Decorative Art*. Oxford: Phaidon.

Greenblatt, Stephen.1998.
Wunderbare Besitztümer. Berlin:
Wagenbach.

Hargittai, István. 1984. "The
Seven One-dimensional Space-
group Symmetries." *Journal of the
Chemical Education* 61(12): 1033–4.

Hargittai, István. 1985. "The
Seventeen Two-dimensional Space-
group Symmetries in Hungarian
Needlework." *Journal of the
Chemical Education* 62(1): 35–6.

Hargittai, István (ed.). 1986.
*Symmetry. Unifying Human
Understanding*. New York: Elsevier
Science.

Hoffman, Donald D. 2000. *Visuelle
Intelligenz*. Stuttgart: Klett-Cotta.

Irmscher, Günter. 1984. *Kleine
Kunstgeschichte des europäischen
Ornaments seit der frühen Neuzeit*.
Darmstadt: Wissenschaftliche
Buchgesellschaft.

Kraft, Kerstin. 2002. "Muster
ohne Wert." http://eldorado.
uni-dortmund.de:8080/FB16/in3/
forschung/2002/Kraft.

Kroll, Frank-Lothar. 1987. *Das Ornament in der Kunsttheorie des 19. Jahrhunderts*. Hildesheim/Zürich/New York: Olms.

Leroi-Gourhan, André. 1971. *L'homme et la matière*. Paris: Albin-Michel.

Leroi-Gourhan, André. 1973. *Milieu et Techniques*. Paris: Albin-Michel.

Lewin, Roger. 1993. *Komplexitätstheorie*. Hamburg: Hoffmann & Campe.

Mainzer, Klaus. 1988. *Symmetrie der Natur*. Berlin/New York: Gruyter.

Maturana, Humberto L. 1998. *Biologie der Realität*. Frankfurt am Main: Suhrkamp.

McAllister, James W. 1996. *Beauty and Revolution in Science*. Ithaca, NY: Cornell University Press.

Meinhardt, Hans. 1997. *Wie Schnecken sich in Schale werfen* (*The Algorithmic Beauty of Sea Shells*). Berlin/Heidelberg/New York: Springer Verlag.

Riegl, Alois. 1923. *Stilfragen*. Berlin.

Rutt, Richard. 1987. *A History of Hand Knitting*. London: Independent Publishing Group.

Seiler-Baldinger, Annemarie. 1994. *Textiles. A Classification of Techniques*. Bathurst: Smithsonian.

Stewart, Ian and Martin Golubitsky. 1993. *Denkt Gott symmetrisch?* Basel: Birkhäuser Verlag.

Stewart, Ian. 1998. *Die Zahlen der Natur (Nature's Numbers)*. Heidelberg/Berlin: Spektrum Verlag.

Washburn, Dorothy K. and Donald W. Crowe. 1988. *Symmetries of Culture*. Seattle, WA: University of Washington Press.

Werner, Brad and Mark Kessler. 2003. "Self-organization and Sorted Pattern Ground." *Science* 299: 380–3.

Wersin, Wolfgang von. 1953. *Das elementare Ornament und seine Gesetzlichkeit*. Ravensburg: Maier.

Weyl, Hermann. 1955. *Symmetrie*. Basel/Stuttgart: Birkhäuser Verlag.

Wilson, Eva. 1996. *Ornamente. Das Handbuch einer 8000 jährigen Geschichte (8000 Years of Ornament—An Illustrated Handbook of Motifs)*. Bern/Stuttgart/Wien: Paul Haupt Verlag.

Digital Clothes: Active, Dynamic, and Virtual Textiles and Garments

Abstract

This article will examine the probable and possible pitfalls offered to consumers and designers by the potential of textiles and garments that are responsive, active, interactive, and aware, using technologies inherited from other craft fields such as medical sensing and information technology.

These developments present obvious, and much discussed, opportunities for the design of functional garments for applications in dangerous industries, sports, rescue, and the military. However, the effect on the already complex dynamic between garment and everyday wear has not been so well examined. Using the social effects of the uptake of other now ubiquitous technology devices such as mobile phones and the Internet as a model for social impact, this article will take a look into the possible near future to see both what is possible, but also what can go *wrong* with active garment fashion.

This examination of the "digital" in garment manufacture moves well beyond the current, often rather clumsy incorporation of wires, sensors, and novelty "glow in the dark" fiber optics into conventional clothes. Rather, it examines the maturing of a field in which revolutionary display technologies and bio-feedback sensing are merging with textiles to produce totally natural feeling and looking fabrics that can not only change their overall color, but can display complex patterns, as well as respond to stimuli from wearer and environment. Aspects such as the effects on personal health, social conventions, and economic costs will be considered.

The article will also consider the domain of clothing and fashion for people who inhabit "virtual" environments, interacting with other people in real time. Unlike more familiar computer games, these online environments involve extensive, long-term social interaction between participants. Unfortunately, the choice of "costume" for the visual representation of each player, currently very limited, has become a frustration for individuals, and threatens to limit the social agency and growth of these environments. The problems of designing and implementing credible and engaging fashions for virtual reality are therefore also examined.

ANNE FARREN AND ANDREW HUTCHISON

Anne Farren is coordinator of the Fashion and Textiles Design course in the Department of Design at Curtin University of Technology, Perth, Western Australia. Her experience includes significant curatorial and cultural exchange projects. Her practice encompasses fashion, textiles, art, and design and she was a convenor of The space between conference, Perth, Western Australia, April 2004, as well as a curator of the parallel exhibition of the same name.

Andrew Hutchison is a researcher in the area of the impact of media technology on narrative, art, and fashion. He is a lecturer in the department of Design at Curtin University of Technology, Perth, Western Australia. He is a multiple-award winning artist in the area of new media. He is one of the curators of The space between exhibition at the John Curtin Gallery, Curtin University of Technology, Perth, Western Australia in April 2004.

Opposite page: photograph of optical camouflage jacket, Tachi Laboratory, University of Tokyo.

Textile, Volume 2, Issue 3, pp. 290–307
Reprints available directly from the Publishers.

Digital Clothes: Active, Dynamic, and Virtual Textiles and Garments

Introduction

The digital 1990s have had great impact on the lives of modernized peoples, creating the reality that we can communicate and have presence in ways never before experienced. We e-mail and chat in real time, message and talk from mobile telephones, and have presence and persist in virtual text and image websites. The overall aesthetic of this digital experience manifests itself to us in two distinct ways.

One is based on the technology of the 1960s, the wires, antennae, hard molded plastic, control panels, keyboards, and screens that we find in mobile phones and digital interfaces. The other is that of the virtual presence, either in disembodied text, or the three-dimensionally rendered virtual worlds of computer games that have become an icon of the late twentieth century. However, an inevitable human desire has seen the beginnings of a merging of these plastic, metal, and silicon technologies with the more intimate, tactile textures and social functions of garments and textiles.

The potential of textiles and garments that are responsive, active, interactive, and aware now presents itself, using technologies inherited from other craft fields such as medical sensing and information technology. This area of investigation has been pursued to a significant extent in the area known as "wearable technologies." However, this article assumes the maturing of a field in which revolutionary software and display/sensing technologies are merging with textiles to produce totally natural feeling and/or looking fabrics that can not only change their overall color, but can display complex patterns, as well as respond to stimuli from wearer and environment, both in the real world, and the virtual. The intersection of digital technologies with textiles is changing the relationship between garment and the body.

This article will consider first the effects of digital technologies on the tangible, actual real world of textiles, garment, and the body, and then explore the social significance of clothes in virtual worlds.

Tangible Digital Textiles and Garments

The Italian company Luminex has produced a novel fabric that includes a special fiber-optic strand that allows garments to glow visibly in reduced lighting conditions (Figure 1). It is already possible to purchase battery-powered tablecloths, handbags, and "mini-tops" from their online store (Luminex 2003). The key feature of Luminex products is that they literally shine, emitting

Figure 1
Luminex fabric garment.
Photo property of Luminex S.p.A.

Figure 2
Garment incorporating Luminex fabric, Susan Taber Avila (model Carrie Simms).

light (Figure 2). This product range illustrates the potential adapted from information technologies, but it also depends upon novelty, rather than function, for most of its application at the present time. There are immediate and obvious uses in safety, entertainment, and interior design, but it seems less applicable to everyday wear.

It is an unusual occasion or event in which you want an article of clothing to look like a Christmas tree.

Another alternative product being developed is International Fashion Machines' Electric Plaid (International Fashion Machines 2003). While International Fashion Machines (IFM) have also experimented with the inclusion of luminous light points in garments (the Firefly dress), it is their Electric Plaid that seems to offer a revolution in the way we think about garments, and how they appear (Figure 3). It has taken the critical step beyond the novelty and limited application of "glow in the dark," and realized that the true potential of a merging of fashion and textiles design with digital/information technologies is in the control of clothes that do not appear to be novel, that work in normal lighting conditions, are under full control by the wearer, and lend themselves to subtle aesthetic variations.

Electric Plaid offers an exciting example of the potential aesthetic of future fabrics. Its fundamental principle is color-changing dyes that are incorporated into a fabric with normal weight, drape and handle. It looks and feels like a normal fabric, already suitable for interior design uses, with two very significant characteristics. First, it does not emit light, like a television screen or fiber-optic system. It reflects whatever light falls on it, thus producing a completely normal optical effect. Secondly, it is capable of changing color not just dependent on some circumstantial environmental factor, such as humidity or temperature, but under specific and reproducible control. It can also already display changing, specific patterns. Both these characteristics are extremely important. The early, current versions of Electric Plaid fabrics are still only suitable for interior design applications, rather than garment construction, since they are still restricted in their physical weight and power supply needs. However, both the Luminex and IFM fabrics present very compelling evidence that everyday wearable color and pattern-changing fabrics are possibly very close indeed.

Figure 3
Electric Plaid, IFM.

The media and information technology industries call any device that can reproduce a variable, stored image a display system. The most familiar to us are the projected movie image, and the television-computer screen. These systems suffer from a large number of drawbacks, including the need for low light environments, weight, power use, physical inflexibility, poor resolution and color reproduction, and speed with which the image can change. A great deal of research is underway to develop display systems that solve all of these problems, for various applications. LED and plasma display television screens are examples of improvements in very recent times, solving problems of weight, size and power use. However, much more radical developments are under way. For example, a display system that seems to be paper is in development (McCormick 2000). Instead of carrying a computer, or reading a disposable newspaper, the user simply unfolds the "paper," and uploads the current text they want to read (E Ink 2003). Other researchers are developing the systems to generate electricity directly from body heat (Baard 2001), or to pass digital information directly over the skin (Williamson and Iliopoulos 2001), and this would do away with the weight, cost, fragility, and, most importantly, the aesthetic, of electrical devices. It seems obvious that with this amount of research under way, the wearable fabric/textile display system that will enable garment construction as fashion designers understand it now will be brought about by a

combination of technologies we can already see emerging. While "intelligent fashion" is not as yet on the catwalk, the integration of digital technology into garment is a reality for the "fashion techies" (Quinn 2002: 97). It is a trend that the fashion designer will need to embrace at some point, and the explorations made by those working in digital technologies are already impacting on notions of "garment."

The Base Garment Concept

The realization that these fabric technologies are realistic possibilities leads us to suggest the concept of the "base garment." Such a garment, say a jacket or pair of trousers, would have a default color of black. The wearer would determine the color by a control in a garment component such as pocket or button, or a wireless accessory such as brooch, necklace or earrings. Indeed, such a digital control device could easily be incorporated into the software of the most recent mobile phones.

Standard industry mobile device communications protocols such as Bluetooth (Bluetooth 2003) are emerging that allow almost any digital device to communicate with any other, and this ease of movement is of course one of the fundamental advantages of digital information. Mobile phones are such devices, and the recent incorporation of still-image and video-capable cameras to mobile phones demonstrates the evolution of the mobile phone into the hand-held, all-purpose digital media device.

Using the control device, the wearer could simply choose

the color they want the base garment to be. Thus, the need for multiple colors of essentially the same garment is overcome. The garment's color could be changed during the day, or even be preprogrammed to slowly change color in response to changing environmental conditions, such as indoor lighting or daylight. Such a garment would also have the capacity to change its pattern, as well as its overall color. This could be familiar patterns, such as houndstooth or tartans, which are generated from the principles of weaving themselves, but since the garment could display *any* pattern, the creative options for textiles designers open up, including patterns that actually animate. This presents the opportunity for a garment that is immediately variable from branded to generic, from subtle shades to flamboyant patterning (Figure 4).

This may seem far-fetched, but everyday wear is already characterized by the presence of logos and typographic elements, and the relationship between typography and motion graphics is already an old one in the media industry. When the technology to make images move is available, image are made to move, wherever they are in the media landscape.

This potential is extended by the inclusion of surveillance and biomedical devices and principles. Prototypes of systems already exist for the gathering of data such as stress levels, breathing rates, blood pressure, and pulse (Picard and Healey 1999). Originally developed for military application, the "smart shirt" has opened the door to the integration of

Figure 4
Optical camouflage jacket, Tachi
Laboratory, University of Tokyo.

comprehensive communications
and monitoring systems into
garments (O'Mahony 2002).
The close proximity of everyday
garments to the skin makes them
ideal carriers for such sensors, and
it is feasible to include these data
as a source to generate patterns
of display on the base garment.
Video images from micro-cameras
incorporated into clothes could be
used to "reflect" the environment
around, and indeed, this principle
has been demonstrated already
(Inami and Kawakami 2003), and
is under investigation for military
use as "active" and "optical"
camouflage. While there remain
enormous technical problems
for military systems where the
non-detectability of the system
is critical (McCarthy 2003),
applications in everyday wear
will not have the same burden of
avoiding being obvious.

While all of these things are
technically feasible, it is far from
clear how they would actually
be used in day-to-day living. For
example, such garments would
make it possible to watch television
on the sleeve of your jacket, or
to cheat in exams by reading the
textbook that appears on the
trouser leg in your lap. Children
might play games where they
upload more and more outlandish
variations of patterns to each
other's base garments.

The Implications

The positive implications of this
base garment are potentially
very significant. The social and
economic impact of the variable
and digital nature of such an
artifact can be seen immediately
with lessons from the digital
industries. One of the reasons
for the astonishing growth of
Microsoft and other software
companies is that they do not
make anything except software.
Such companies do not need to

invest in heavy industrial capital, and their products only weigh as much as the packaging materials they are wrapped in and carried on. The software industry is about intellectual property, not the physical artifact.

If we extend this realization to the business of fabric and garment design, we can see that designers could produce innovative and experimental work that could be distributed not as finished products, but as a few kilobytes of information, for wearers to download to their mobile phones and then upload to their base garments. The creative end of garment and cloth making would be to some extent disconnected from structural and decorative limitations of printing and weaving technologies. New looks could move as fast as e-mail and text messages. Cycles of fashion change could be dramatically accelerated. Seasons could become only a few days long, particularly in social settings where trends move more quickly.

However, further concerns immediately arise when modeling the possible impact of base garments with software-determined colors and patterns. The fashion and garment retail industry performs some role in deciding what styles people will have access to, and in this capacity they are "arbiters of good taste." While the potential has always been available to those who choose to make their own clothes to do so, the base garment frees them from the process of actual garment construction. The freedom to design and publish will move into the hands of individuals not

trained in the industry. While this will offend many professional designers, it will demonstrate the extent to which training/industrial institutions delimit the look of what we wear. A similar phenomenon occurred during the late 1980s and early 1990s, when the emergence of computers in the print media area demonstrated that much of what had previously been considered to be graphic design was in fact just "desk-top publishing." The craft was changed and reoriented accordingly.

Imagine an entire shopping mall or café where every jacket and pair of trousers is animating or changing color. This visual pollution, in which it seems many inner urban landscapes already suffer some form of advertising or branding on every available surface, could be even worse if the owners of base garments sold the rights to advertise on their clothes. The technological means to do so already exist, via mobile phone networks.

While this kind of scenario seems bad enough, if we invoke another unexpected and unwanted phenomenon from the information age, it gets worse. E-mail viruses are a deliberate misuse of the inherent capacity of digital information to be spread and implemented easily. The "computer hacker" phenomenon has demonstrated that if an information technology system can be tampered with, it will be, and the same would undoubtedly occur with software-distributed styles, colors, and patterns. In the same way that viruses work now, they could have an immediate impact in the everyday wear media-scape,

such as turning all garments in an area the exact same color or pattern at a predetermined time, or causing graffiti or obscenities to animate across people's clothes. The potential yield for the hacker, in embarrassment caused, or social commentary made at a public event, is far greater than the same impact on computer users, since it is so much more visual and public.

There has been little discussion of the potential electromagnetic hazards of such garments. The risk of being electrocuted by your clothes is not the issue here. Such a risk is so obvious, and the design principles to avoid it are so well established, that it is very difficult to imagine it occurring. However, there is a whole aspect of electromagnetic radiation (as opposed to nuclear radiation) risk to the body that is not well understood by science.

The short-term dangers of being close to high-energy radio waves, microwaves, and radars are known, but there is much community concern, anecdotal evidence, and lingering scientific uncertainty about what the *long-term* effects on the human body are of exposure to *relatively low*-energy radiation (World Health Organization 2003). Over the course of the twentieth century, all humans in densely populated areas have been subject to an increasing level of radio waves passing through their bodies, produced by radio and television stations, airport radar, military and emergency service radio communications systems, radio "noise" from the rotating parts of electric motors, high-voltage power lines, etc. The explosion of mobile telephone networks has increased the amount of such energy passing through every human body. In addition, mobile phone usage offers a unique added risk because the inherent consequence of the compact design of mobile phones is that the radio transmitter is positioned directly near the head in order to use the microphone and ear speaker. It is the very intimacy of garments that makes this potential risk so great.

Uncertainty over these risks is due to the very nature of the possible problem, i.e. low levels over a long period of time (Brewin and Disabatino 2000). Nevertheless, it may be a discovery of the mid-twenty-first century that the risks are significant or even serious, and that the human body is affected in subtle ways by such electromagnetic radiation exposure (Beal 2004). Given this possibility, the prospect of literally dressing ourselves in digital garments that generate power from our body, pass information through our skin, emit and receive constant information from other devices nearby, or generate such radiation as a side effect of the technique they use to change color and pattern, becomes of concern. However, the solution may lie in the garment itself. One of the applications of new technology fabrics is to shield the body from the effects of electromagnetic radiation (Manabu 2002).

The active, dynamic, and variable nature of garments in the future will not be limited just to those technologies that we currently lump together under the term "digital." "Nano-tech" is a term just as ill-defined as

"digital," and inevitably is, and will be, used in the same way to describe a whole variety of techniques related not just by their technical underpinning, but because they are associated with each other in time or application. Nano-technology offers the possibility that another variable aspect of base garments will be their physical shape and size. New technology fabrics and textiles with variable length and in-built sensors might allow garments to auto-fit the wearer's basic physical dimensions, reducing the number of sizes that garments needed to be manufactured in. If so, then for the first time in history "large," "medium," and "small" might actually work for everyone. It would then be a small extra step to afford the wearer the ability to modify the exact length or cut of garments to suit particular combinations or circumstances. Such garments have been imagined in fiction for years, perhaps most conspicuously in the movie *Back to the Future 2* (1989), where the hero's jacket automatically fits to his size when he puts it on, and also has an automatic drying mechanism in case it becomes wet. In fact, this late-1980s film was far too conservative in its imaginings of the future, since "nano-tech" fabrics already exist that will not need to self-dry, because they are chemically *incapable* of becoming wet, as a result of their molecular makeup (Mecia 2002). Fabrics that literally self-clean as they become dirty, while they are worn, have been proposed as a potential stemming from nano-biotechnologies (University of Massachusetts 2001). Full-body scanning of customers (Newman 2003) would allow their exact body specifications to be digitally recorded, uploaded, and this information used in a variety of ways in "auto-fitting" such active garments.

A further possible implication for the textile, garment, and fashion industry is the possibility in a dramatic decline in the number of actual garments that will be manufactured. It is obvious that a huge number of garments never actually wear out, but simply become unfashionable to wear, and so must be replaced. If fashion itself could be uploaded to a base garment, especially if it was of variable cut and length as well as color and pattern, then there could be significant impact on the sheer volume of fabric that needs to be manufactured, cut, and constructed. While this might have positive outcomes for the environment, it could also produce a great shift in employment in the textiles industry.

The Lived Experience of Base Garments

There is no question that the combination of digital and associated technologies has the potential to bring about at least some of the visual, physical, and interactive/interconnected characteristics of the "base garments" we have described. But changes do not occur simply because they are technologically feasible. They occur because people find them useful. Mobile phones and e-mail have not swept the developed world because they are digital, but rather because

they massively extend individual people's ability to communicate and connect. They are of social significance. And in this regard, they are like fashion and clothes.

The key reason the base garment concept is so important is because it allows an extension of that which people are already doing with fashion and garments, making choices about what they wear, how they appear, and what that appearance communicates to other people. Pia Myrvold's current work in engaging the customer to participate in the design of their own garment demonstrates the further potential if a combined technology "base garment" system become possible (Quinn 2002).

And in this lies a tension. More variability, more choice, gives an individual not only more control, but more decisions to make. Is part of the value of the fashion industry that it reduces the amount of choice most people need to deal with? Are most people happy to conform with whatever trends are presented in retail outlets?

An inevitable consequence of base garments would be to vary the levels of engagement of individuals concerning the very fine detail of color, color matches, the exact length of hems, etc. More variability means a more complex visual language we would all have to become literate with, and this may become an overwhelming experience. One of the often-quoted advantages of school uniforms is that they eradicate such variances and choices from the school environment, with near-adult students and parents less distracted by the financial, social, and practical problems of

deciding what to wear. Of course, many teenagers resent this, and find ways to corrupt the uniform, particularly with accessories. The desire to individualize, or at least be identified as current in a particular group, is at odds with the desire to be unburdened about what to wear on any given day, and whether or not it is appropriate. If we imagine base garments introduced into the context of the school uniform, we can see that it not only increases the number of ways for the uniform to be corrupted, but it also allows students to immediately change the uniform as they step off the school grounds, implementing their own variations to the uniform to creating their group's own sub-identity, or completely dispensing with the uniform altogether while they engage in the time-honored and socially critical experience of "hanging around" in conspicuous locations. This notion of the base garment contributes to the discussion by Quinn (2003) of garment as a dwelling and the emergence of the "urban nomad." Base garments can be changed and adapted to suit the social, geographic or political environment the wearer finds themselves in.

But this connection to the characteristics of digital media does offer some threats to the very identity of the craft and business of garment and fashion design. Does the integration of technology into the garment result in us becoming "tethered" to the Internet (O'Mahony 2002)? It seems possible that garment design is at risk of becoming simply a vehicle for information technology software or hardware sales.

Initiatives such as Sensotech and Technolust (Lupton 2002) illustrate that the integration between technology and garment remains primarily driven by the "fashion techies." While this is the case, the concerns of fashion and garment design will remain secondary to the development of consumer electronics. Authors such as Quinn (2002) and O'Mahony (2002) point out the need for fashion, communications, and information technology to forge mutually beneficial alliances.

Virtual Digital

If the potential of real-world flexible display devices and color-changing fabrics opens up whole new opportunities, then the possibilities that appear for designers and wearers in the virtual realms are even more unlimited.

The development in the 1990s of advanced special effects for movies and television rapidly followed the developing speed of computer technology. By the very late 1990s the sophistication of this craft had resulted in the capacity to realistically (as perceived by the average person) reproduce the drape, handle, and movement of real fabrics on a moving body, as perhaps most conspicuously illustrated in *Shrek* (2001) and *Star Wars: Attack of the Clones* (2002). While *Shrek*'s characters and their clothes were completely produced in a virtual world (with the exception of the character's voices), *Star Wars* went one step further and composited real actors with real costumes and virtual characters with virtual clothes together in one

scene. As the two characters move around, their clothes seemingly change shape in response to their movement, and the wind. The significance of this is that virtual technologies are capable of matching real clothes in their behavior, albeit on screen. It is this kind of advance that incrementally moves virtual characters from looking like dolls to looking more like credible humans. Jane Harris's projected video art works such as *Potential Beauty* (2003) highlight these techniques in abstract form, and indicate just how realistic virtual fabrics can be (Figure 5).

These capabilities appear in Hollywood films before they appear in computer games because the sheer computer power needed is too expensive for the domestic consumer, the software for these virtual creations is often written specifically for the movie, and the techniques are often previously untried. However, the development of three-dimensional modeling and rendering generally shows us that it is only months, rather than years, before a similar or same level of capability appears in the retail "games" market, and so we can expect that it will be sooner, rather than later, that these sophisticated advances will appear in "online" virtual worlds. The rapid growth rates of capabilities in the digital area are likely to be reflected in virtual generation of textile and garment.

For fashion and textile designers, such application offers the opportunity to design without limitation caused by the physical characteristics or comfort of the wearer, the limitations of materials technologies or costs.

Figure 5
Potential Beauty, Jane Harris.

This presents the opportunity to explore ideas and implementations of ideas in the virtual world without material or construction costs. While the impracticality of catwalk fashion for everyday use is often noted, in virtual worlds, not only could the designs be even *more* outlandish, they could be worn all day by virtual characters.

Already, hundreds of thousands of people have virtual lives in online gaming environments that are far more like communities than conventional video games. What makes them more like real life, and less like games, is that people take on an identity of their own, choosing and developing their character over time (months or years), often in ongoing relationships with other real people's characters. It is extremely social. All of these communities involve the player taking on a visual identity, the avatar. A current problem is that the range of options for what a player can look like is very limited. You have to choose from a set of items.

A good example of such an online game with this problem is *EverQuest* (1999), a role-playing game with a "dungeons and dragons," "sword and the sorcerer" fantasy theme. A researcher studying *EverQuest* (Klastrup 2003) has described her "quest for pants" as a player. Choosing to be a female human character, she was confronted with the discovery that the way her character appeared to other players was as a long-legged, big-breasted Amazon warrior stereotype, wearing a "g-string" or "thong" rather than trousers, skirt or dress. Klastrup discovered that she could buy clothing items in the game world, but upon buying some pants, she discovered that although the pants appeared in her list of belongings, they did not appear on her avatar, and so she remained dressed in a manner she was not comfortable with. This was finally resolved by her undertaking a very special quest during which she captured special magical armor (with pants) which, since it was a part of the designed story, did appear on her avatar (Figure 6).

Klastrup's experience illustrates the very real limitations that such environments present to participants in these "games," which in fact have a long-term social significance. People want to be able to be in control of their appearance, even in a virtual world, because of what it signals to others, and to one's self. It reaffirms our understanding that how we dress is fundamental to our identity. Designers of these worlds will need to address these issues in order to maintain their relevance to a broad community. Given that the rate at which the movie industry's techniques are becoming available to the designers and players of such online games, it would seem reasonable to assume that the ability to choose highly unique combinations and variations of clothes (and other visual attributes such as hair length and color) will quickly appear in environments

Figure 6
Clothes on virtual characters in *EverQuest*.

such as *EverQuest*, and indeed this development seems so natural since we have an expectation that virtual worlds will provide limitless opportunities.

However, the future may not be so bright. In the same way that on-line gaming communities need to be more socially real to make them attractive, they may also take on the negative aspects of real social worlds. The novel *Snow Crash* (Stephenson 1992) is set in a world where persistent virtual environments are commonplace, and it describes a situation where fashion items remain economically determined, through technological limitation. In the virtual world of *Snow Crash*, wealthy people can afford expensive, custom-designed avatars implemented by expert programmers and powered by unlimited bandwidth. In the same virtual world, merely normal people have to put up with cheap, mass-produced, black-and-white, low-resolution generic avatars, and so their avatar is identical to most other people's in the virtual world. They walk down the same streets, observing and being observed, just as in the real world. And so we see the familiar divide between "chain store" fashion on one hand, and "high" designer label fashion on the other.

This possible future scenario already has a current manifestation. Players in virtual communities are at a social disadvantage if they have a slower computer, or a slower bandwidth link to the server that physically hosts the data of the virtual world. This delay, called "lag," may mean that other players seem aloof, stupid or completely unaware of

you, or that action has arisen and transpired before a player can engage in it. This lag issue is not a minor technical point. It is in fact a highly determining factor in real-time social interaction online. Although there is no theoretical reason why a player could not play with people from anywhere on the face of the real earth, in fact most players play with people who live relatively geographically close. This is partly because of language barriers, and time zones, but also because lag time is generally less inside a region than between regions. This problem will become even more serious with advancing expectations of the quality of audiovisual rendering of avatars and their clothes. More audio and higher quality, more realistic, smoother animating graphics will require not only much more powerful computers for each player, but much more bandwidth. A simple way to overcome the lag problem is to get a higher speed link. Of course, this cost more money. Not only that, but the technical infrastructure that hosts the game world the players are connecting to will be under much greater stress, and this will need to be upgraded.

It is already the case that hosting services offer ranges of service based on cost, and so it is easy to see that even though it is technically feasible to provide everyone with equal access to virtual fashions and garments, it is very unlikely to occur. The designers of these game worlds need to make a living, and so will offer their client base a product range and price structure that promotes the higher cost of

technically and creatively rarer objects, a situation we are all familiar with as consumers. Once again, this trend has already been observed. Virtual objects, and even whole characters, from games such as *EverQuest* are being created and then sold in the real world for real money. In fact, the *virtual* money from the games themselves can now be bought and sold with real money in the *real world* at online currency exchanges (Ward 2004). In such a context, it seems very likely that as soon as the game designers include the technical capacity for variable, customizable textiles and garments, fashion designers will begin the creation and selling of boutique lines and *haute couture*.

While the particular example of *EverQuest* is explicitly set in a fantasy world where humans, magic, and monsters coexist, there are other, even more popular virtual environments that are based directly on real life. *Sims Online* (2002) is an online, multi-user, persistent world not significantly different from the contemporary consumer world we live in now. It has come under criticism for connecting popularity and/or attractiveness of characters to ownership of consumer goods (SarahR 2003). In such an environment, the potential of customizable clothes is that it fuels a potentially unhealthy pursuit of "brand compliance," in which clothes might be chosen not so people can be different from one another, but so they can have membership of the same "brand" identity. Major, actual, fashion labels have already licensed the rights to their brands to game world designers, selling branded virtual clothes for real money (Takahashi 2003).

In this way, such virtual worlds might become less a fanciful escape from real life, and more a reductive continuation of real-world consumption. In this case, fashion may play the same important role in both the real world and the virtual, prescribing both possibilities and limitations on both the designers and the consumers.

Conclusion

This article has necessarily encompassed both the real, tangible world that we physically touch and the increasingly common virtual worlds, not only because of the broad meaning of the term "digital," but also because what happens in "virtual" worlds is only virtual in one very narrow sense. The very attraction of online gaming communities, and what makes them startlingly different from all other computer and video games, is that they are explicitly about social interaction with other, real people. The social experience people have in virtual worlds is still a real experience had by a real person. The flamboyant, physically impossible, fantasy garment worn or observed in a "virtual" experience is really experienced nonetheless.

Real, tangible base garments would increase the capacity to vary the way we appear in the real world, but would this increase the tension between individual identity and practical convenience, or relieve it? The answer is probably "yes" in some circumstances and in others, probably "no." A

world with ubiquitous variable base garments would be, like the world we now have with ubiquitous mobile phones, neither better nor worse than before, just different. And whether or not spending significant time in virtual circumstances might reduce or increase the need for individuals to self-express with fashion, or to define their conformity, membership or individuality, is something that this article cannot anticipate.

What is clear though is that our twentieth-century notions of the digital will be rapidly transformed by the development of technology we have not yet experienced. The twenty-first century will not be dominated by the twentieth-century "digital," any more than the twentieth century was dominated by the steam engines or weaving looms of the nineteenth century. Both the virtual and tangible garment possibilities we have described here are feasible, and will present the textiles, garment, and fashion industries with new challenges and opportunities. The integration of digital media into garments, and of garments into digital media, gives rise to a literal manifestation of the "skins" for the body that have a "life of their own," described by Lupton (2002). Like the clothes we wear now, these constructs that assist and support the human wearer are both essential, and essentially alien, to the human condition.

References
Baard, Erik. 2001. "People Power: Capturing the Body's Energy for Work on and off Earth." www.

space.com/businesstechnology/ technology/body_power_011128- 1.html, accessed December 20 2003.

Back to the Future 2. 1989. Robert Zemeckis (dir.). Universal Pictures.

Beal, James. 2004. "Definition of Electromagnetic Field Sensitivity Syndrome (EMFSS)." *Electromagnetic Radiation.* http:// canterbury.cyberplace.org.nz/emr/ beal2.html, accessed January 12 2004.

Bluetooth. 2003. http://www. bluetooth.com/, accessed November 22 2003.

Brewin, Bob and Jennifer Disabatino. 2000. "Are Companies Liable for Cell-phone Health Risks?" www.cnn.com/2000/TECH/ computing/08/02/cell.phone. liability.idg/index.html, accessed January 10 2004.

E Ink 2003. "E Ink and Philips to Show Advanced Paper-like Display Prototypes." http://eink. com/news/releases/pr69.html, accessed November 18 2003.

EverQuest. 1999. Online role playing game. Sony On-line. http://everquest.station.sony. com/.

Inami, Masahiko and Naoki Kawakami. 2003. "Optical Camouflage." *X'tal Vision.* http:// www.star.t.u-tokyo.ac.jp/projects/ MEDIA/xv/oc.html, accessed January 14 2004.

International Fashion Machines. 2003. "Electric Plaid." http://www. ifmachines.com/pinkrotate.html, accessed August 27 2003.

Klastrup, Lisbeth. 2003. "A Poetics of Virtual Worlds." Verbal report in

paper presented at MelbourneDAC, the 5th International Digital Arts and Culture Conference, May 19–23 2003, School of Applied Communication, RMIT, Melbourne, Australia.

Luminex. 2003. http://www. luminex.it/, accessed August 18 2003.

Lupton, Ellen. 2002. *Skin: Surface, Substance, and Design.* Princeton, NJ: Princeton Architectural Press.

Manabu, Yoshino. 2002. "Development and Evaluation of the Electromagnetic Shielding Knitted Clothing." *Bulletin of Tokyo Metropolitan Industrial Technology Research Institute* No. 5 (November 2002). http://www.iri.metro.tokyo. jp/publish/report/14/ea26.html, accessed January 15 2004.

Mecia, Tony. 2002. "Ailing Burlington Textile Company Pins its Hopes on Nanotech." *Smalltimes: Big News in Small Tech.* http:// www.smalltimes.com/document_ display.cfm?document_id=5230, accessed January 28 2004.

McCarthy, Wil. 2003. " Being Invisible." *Wired* 11(8) http://www. wired.com/wired/archive/11.08/ pwr_invisible.html, accessed January 20 2004.

McCormick, Gavin. 2000. "E Ink Ties with Lucent to Speed E- books." http://boston.internet. com/news/article.php/393581, accessed December 23 2003.

Newman, Cathy. 2003. "Dreamweavers." *National Geographic* January 2003: 51–73.

O'Mahony, Marie. 2002. Cyborg: The Man-Machine. London: Thames & Hudson.

Picard, Rosalind, and Jennifer Healey. 1999. "Prototype of an Affective Wearable Computer." *Affective Wearables.* http://www. white.media.mit.edu/tech-reports/ TR-467/node4.html, accessed December 15 2003.

Potential Beauty. 2003. Projected video art work. Jane Harris.

Quinn, Bradley. 2002. *Techno Fashion.* Oxford: Berg.

——. 2003. *The Fashion of Architecture.* Oxford: Berg.

SarahR. 2003. "Virtual Chaos." *futureStep | net.tech, academia, society & culture on-line news group.* http://fania.oit.duke. edu/weblog_archive/000131.html, accessed January 28 2004.

Shrek. 2001. Dreamworks.

Sims Online. 2002. Electronic Arts.

Stephenson, Neal. 1992. *Snow Crash.* London: Bantam Spectra.

Star Wars: Attack of the Clones. 2002. George Lucas (dir.). 20th Century Fox/LucasFilm.

Takahashi. Dean. "New Virtual World Being Launched." *Silicon Valley.com: Inside the Tech Economy.* http://www.siliconvalley. com/mld/siliconvalley/7113913. htm, accessed January 28 2004.

University of Massachusetts. 2001. "Self-cleaning Clothing? UMass Dartmouth Engineering Professor's Research Makes it Likely." *The Observer at University of Massachusetts, Darmouth* 11(1). http://www.umassd.edu/ communications/publications/ observer/06_2001/selfcleaning. cfm, accessed January 28 2004.

Ward, Mark. 2004. "Virtual Cash Exchange Goes Live." *BBC News: Technology.* http://news.bbc.co.uk/2/hi/technology/3368633.stm, accessed January 2004.

Williamson, Adrian and Constantinos Iliopoulos. 2001. "The Learning Organization Information System (LOIS): Looking for the Next Generation." *Information Systems Journal* 11(1): 23.

World Health Organization. 2003. "Summary of Health Effects: What Happens When You Are Exposed to Electromagnetic Fields?" http://www.who.int/peh-emf/about/WhatisEMF/en/index1.html, accessed January 10 2004.

Textiles, Patterns, and Technology: Digital Tools for the Geometric Analysis of Cloth and Culture

Abstract

Advances in information technology now provide a variety of digital tools for the mathematical investigation of the visual complexity of textile patterns and decorative designs. In this article, we report on innovative applications of this technology to the geometric analysis of Kuba cloth and Zillij mosaics. From our perspective, these objects present distinctly different analytical challenges, and typify problematic aspects of the classification and generation problems of artistic design. Mathematical considerations led us to use neural networks, shape grammars, and related technologies to approach these problems. Our ultimate goal is to use our methods, samples, and peripherals to build an interactive database for the study of historical patterns and the generation of contemporary designs. Details of our research plan can be found in Kolak Dudek *et al.* 2003: 129–35).

SUSHIL BHAKAR, CHERYL KOLAK DUDEK, SYLVAIN MUISE, LYDIA SHARMAN, ERIC HORTOP AND FRED E. SZABO

Sushil Bhakar is a PhD student in computer science at Concordia University in Montreal. His research interests are three-dimensional computational graphics and visualization. His part-time hobbies include abstract algebra, mathematical logic, and their applications. Currently, he is working on two research projects: real-time point-based rendering of three-dimensional objects and the mathematical structure of patterns such as the geometry underlying Kuba cloths and Zillij mosaics.

Eric Hortop is a double-major co-op student in mathematics, statistics, and communication studies at Concordia University in Montreal, with a minor in fine arts. He is an accomplished problem-solver and plans to continue on in research and envisages a career in academia or government. His other interests include computers, graphic design, typography, cooking, and long-distance bicycling.

Cheryl Kolak Dudek is an associate professor of Print Media in the Studio Arts Department at Concordia University in Montreal. She holds a Doctorate of Arts degree in contemporary criticism from New York University and a Master of Fine Arts in printmaking from Columbia University. She has taught at the University of Virginia, Denison University, and Princeton University, where she was a visiting artist for three years. Her artwork has been exhibited internationally in numerous solo and group shows and is in the public collections of IBM, the Brooklyn Museum, the New York Public Library and Zejiang Academy of Fine Arts in Hangzhou. She is a member of Hexagram: Institute of Research and Creation in Media Arts and Technologies in Montreal.

Sylvain Muise is an undergraduate co-op student in pure and applied mathematics at Concordia University in Montreal. He has extensive experience in computer programming, image processing, web design, and database management. His current research focus is on the development of an interactive database for graphic art. Sylvain's other interests include music and the visual interpretation of sound.

Lydia Sharman is Professor of Design in the Faculty of Fine Arts at Concordia University in Montreal. She has worked extensively with the geometry of design, including her doctoral research on symbolism in traditional Islamic pattern and ornament, and has exhibited her prints and photography internationally. As an educator, she has developed programs on mathematics in Islamic art in Canada, the United States, and the United Kingdom, in both Muslim and non-Muslim communities. Her publications on the subject include *Teaching Math through Islamic Art* (Sharman 1994), a publication by the Victoria and Albert Museum, London, and *The Amazing Book of Shapes* (Sharman 1996), which has been translated into Dutch, Greek, German, Hebrew, Catalan, and Castilian. She is a member of Hexagram: Institute of Research and Creation in Media Arts and Technologies in Montreal.

Fred E. Szabo is Professor of Mathematics at Concordia University in Montreal. He has studied philosophy, politics, and economics at Oxford University, and holds a PhD in mathematics from McGill University in Montreal. For the last ten years, he has directed the cooperative programs in Mathematics, Statistics, and Actuarial Science. Before that, he was Dean of the School of Graduate Studies where he successfully supported interdisciplinary studies and research at Concordia University. In addition to his publications in mathematics, he has written extensively on contemporary issues in higher education. He has contributed to several Educational Leadership Seminars, has represented Canada at NAFTA conferences, and is currently active in collaborative research linking mathematics, technology, and the visual arts.

Textile, Volume 2, Issue 3, pp. 308–327
Reprints available directly from the Publishers.

Textiles, Patterns, and Technology: Digital Tools for the Geometric Analysis of Cloth and Culture

Background

Geometric Patterns in Ethnomathematics

Geometric patterns in African Kuba cloth are fractured and reiterated in an astounding display of improvisation that connects the viewer to the artisan in a special dialogue. Women embroider, stitch, and cut raffia pile into velvet patterns on a woven raffia base prepared by the men. Confounding traditional notions of geometric symmetry and repetition, Kuba women design their textiles freely as they work, without drawings, over a period of months and sometimes years (Adams 1973: 35). These distinctive monochromatic velvets come from the Kasai-Sankuru river region in central Africa, where Western anthropologists, impressed with the cultural richness of carvings and textiles, have visited the multi-ethnic Kuba kingdom for research and study since the end of nineteenth century.

Fractal symmetry, including recursion, scaling, self-similarity, infinity, and fractal dimension, is displayed in the Kuba designs through juxtapositions of linear embroidery, velvet forms, and contrasting color that becomes counterpunctual in the composition. According to Ron Eglash, fractals are part of African numerical systems as evidenced in their village planning, decorative motifs and textiles. He specifically describes Kuba designs in the computational terms of a complexity spectrum:

These [Kuba designs] tend to show periodic tiling along one axis, and aperiodic tiling—often moving from order to disorder—along the other. Similar geometric visualizations of the spectrum from order to disorder have been used in computer science. As far as I can tell, the Bakuba weavings never reach more than halfway across the spectrum—they are typically moving between 1 and 1.5, that is, from periodic to fractal, rather than stretching all the way to pure disorder. (Eglash 1999: 172–3)

Kuba women create patterns of mathematical complexity and beauty by deviating from static geometric structures with their own personal logic of improvisation. Henri Matisse and Gustav Klimt were both inspired by Kuba design motifs, transforming and referencing the hypergeometric patterns in their paintings. Analogous to the African-American idiom of improvisational jazz, improvisation in Kuba cloth makes their design motifs unique to Western textiles.

It is acknowledged in contemporary theory that aesthetics are a profound manifestation of culture. To recognize that aesthetics are culture bound is a simplification of the complex relationships between belief and knowledge systems, as well as all of the economic-socio-political-historical constructions that define a culture.

When the Whitney Museum of American Art in New York City exhibited the Gee's Bend quilts in 2002, critical acclaim rivaled the quilts to twentieth-century modernist painting. In fact, the quilts were produced over seven decades by a small group of mostly interrelated black women who lived in the isolated and impoverished community of Gee's Bend, Alabama.

Seemingly idiosyncratic, the Gee's Bend quilts do not conform in their geometry to any of the Western quilt traditions. In many cases, they truly are more like paintings because their bold, aggressive, free-form compositions lack the repetitive units of traditionally pieced quilts. Four essays from the exhibition catalog strive to characterize and classify the textiles of Gee's Bend:

Qualities such as multiple patterning and broken patterns, high-effect color contrasts, dissonant juxtapositions of prints or motifs, asymmetry, syncopation, irregular- or random-looking borders, and overall improvisation predominate in the black tradition; while each of these

visual attitudes appears from time to time in nonblack quilts, African American works from throughout the South and the "southern diaspora"—the southern communities to which southern blacks migrated— routinely incorporate all of these strategies, sometimes simultaneously. (Arnett and Arnett 2002: 45)

The Arnetts continue their comments on the materiality of the Gee's Bend quilts:

The strip-construction and free-form-block formats offer a ready tablet for this type of variation, as patterns are modified improvisationally throughout the quilt. Beginning with a regularized strip, subsequent strips might increasingly alter the pattern until the last segment scarcely resembles the first. Such "irregularities" obviously do not result from lack of skill, inattention, or the mandates of poverty. Such elements are full of purpose, not compromise. "Spontaneous" arrangements need to be viewed as an aesthetic philosophy, for they are inseparable from the quiltmakers' sense of overall vision. (Arnett and Arnett 2002: 45)

Although the ethnomathematics of African numerical systems is a relatively new area of research, the geometry and design improvisation of Gee's Bend quilts has been linked to Kuba cloth and the strip-woven textiles of the Ivory Coast and Ghana (Livingston 2002: 53). As indicated earlier, fractal

symmetry, recursion, scaling, self-similarity, and infinity are characteristics of the geometric improvisation found in Kuba cloth, the Gee's Bend quilts, and even improvisational jazz, all African and African-American art forms.

Geometric Patterns in Zillij Mosaics

All traditional patterns are expressions of a culture. For example, the Celts, a people close to the water, have pattern forms based on the two directions of spirals found in the flow of water. Moroccan Zillij mosaics are deeply responsive to the culture, social context, and history of the region. They are a specific expression of an Islamic culture and therefore embody its principles. The traditional view discourages representative art and has led in its place to the development of a very sophisticated mathematical art form that holds many levels of meaning.

The traditional Zillij mosaics have been traced back to the twelfth century and reached a zenith in Fez in the seventeenth century (El-Said and Parman 1976). Some of the best examples are in the madrasahs (universities) in the old Medina. In a small open-fronted shop it is possible to still see three generations involved in the task of making the mosaics: the son making the squares, the father cutting the specific shapes and the grandfather supervising. The mosaics are fired, glazed in colors derived mainly from metals, and then fired again. It is said that to make a Zillij mosaic panel in the traditional way requires great skill and the integration of hand, eye, heart, and mind. Muslims develop their memory and their heart by learning the Qur'ān by heart. A Zillij panel is made by laying each piece in place upside down, then plaster is poured over the back and the pattern is only seen when it is dry. Traditionally, the pattern is conceived by the Master and held in the mind as he lays each piece without seeing the pattern develop. A premise in Islam is that Allah loves beauty, and therefore beauty is a gift to Allah. The Zillij panels with their intense and intricate beauty are found indoors and out, in places of worship, civic buildings, and homes. They also enrich water fountains in a country where this is considered a valuable resource. The example used in this article (see Figure 1) was photographed in a Madrasah in Fez. It has white interwoven lines separating each of the colored mosaic pieces, adding to the intricacy of the pattern. These mosaic panels were used on occasion for contemplation and to focus the mind by following the interwoven lines and by comprehending the beauty and complexity of the geometry of the patterns and the arrangements of color.

The geometric patterns represent a portion of infinity, because in principle the pattern can continue indefinitely in any and all directions. In their great intricacy, they represent diversity in unity and unity in diversity, a vast array of different patterns without individual expression. The geometry encompasses universal, harmonious laws that provide unity within the diversity and beauty of nature—in the arrangements of the petals of a flower, a wasps' nest, or a snowflake.

The geometric figures on which the patterns are based have a symbolic component. All the patterns are based on a circle, the symbol of the infinite without beginning or end and where every part of the line is the same. Patterns are constructed starting with the first theorem of Euclid (Courant and Robbins 1941: 23). After a circle is drawn, the radius is maintained and the compass point is moved to any point on the circumference and a second circle is drawn creating an almond shape in the middle, and the circumference of each circle touches the center of the other. This can represent the first division of the cell, the beginning of life and of polarization, and the number two. The compass point can then be situated on the point on the circumference where the two circles overlap and another circle can be draw. This can go on until six circles fit exactly within the circumference —six circles around a central circle, and two sets of three, as in the petals of many flowers. Three sides makes the simplest polygon. Patterns based on four can be the symbol of materiality—the four directions, and the four states of matter. The pentagon has the ratio of the golden section (the only ratio in which the smaller section is to the greater as the greater section is to the whole), which was referred to as "the divine proportion" by Renaissance writers.

The patterns for the Zillij mosaics are for the most part based on geometric systems that are progressions and multiples of

Figure 1
Kuba cloth from the Congo and
Zillij mosaic from Madrasah, Fez.

figures with three, four, and five equal sides. These in turn have a parallel in music. In the patterns the circle from which all are derived is still evident in the rotational and reflexive symmetry of the center figures. It is this symbolism in the transcendent, geometric patterns of Zillij mosaics that suggests a comprehensive cosmology (Critchlow 1976).

Other Geometric Patterns in Cloth and Culture

Figurative geometric patterns inscribe the surfaces of early Chinese bronze vessels and pre-Columbian Mexican malacates; and are manifested in the designs of Islamic screens and the Irish Book of Kells. At first glance, the tilting geometric pattern with S-shaped dragons from a late Eastern Zhou (fourth century BC) Chinese bronze food container[1] resembles the hooked and angular geometric spirals of a pre-Columbian Xicalcoliuhqui fret.[2] The geometry of other angular spirals, from the Xicalcoliuhqui fret resonates with the zigzags, spirals and lozenges carved into the Newgrange (2500–3200 BC) monuments in Ireland. Coptic (early Egyptian) textiles display geometric patterns of infinity found in Greek meanders and early Chinese bronzes. The spirals, chevrons, step patterns, knots, arabesques, and wave patterns of Celtic art can be found in the geometric designs of many other cultures including Islamic, Chinese, and African.

Assuming that the geometric trace in design motifs is historical and cross cultural, we are developing a database of metapatterns for the mathematical analysis of geometric design. Our project uses methodologies from mathematics and computer science for the analysis, classification, and pattern-generating systems that will comprise our database. We refer to it as the "MetaPattern database." This project is timely for two main reasons: (1) the technology and knowledge for complex and analytical systems is now available; and (2) the MetaPattern database will be an interactive artwork for a generation of new patterns, as well as a resource for historical, archival, cultural, and comparative information about geometric design motifs:

> *Multimedia modeling to harmonize different media and systems is one of the key technologies in the third phase of information processing. It will provide a next generation framework to construct a human-centered information environment that is more comfortable and more productive.* (Hasimoto 2000)

As two- and three-dimensional computer rendering techniques are developed, we have the potential to make very fine distinctions between patterns within the context of a database of cultural, historical and material information.

Digital Tools

Digital computers have revolutionized the modern world. They are used in almost all domains of life. For example, painters now have at their disposal digital tools equivalent to brushes, paints, and erasers. Yet artists do not seem to be completely satisfied with the digital tools currently available. One of the main reasons for this is the gap between the low-level functionalities provided by the software and highly sophisticated level of thinking and working of artists. When artists think of painting a park scene, for example, they may be thinking of children, mothers, balls, swings, and so on, whereas the digital tools available to them allow them only to work at a much lower level with lines, circles, and rectangular shapes. One of the aims of this project is to provide artists with digital tools based on the required higher level of patterns. In this article, we analyze two sources of such patterns: Kuba cloth and Zillij mosaics. Specifically, we want to automate, in part, the discovery of high-level patterns in Kuba cloth and Zillij mosaics. Figure 1 shows examples of both.

In their celebrated analysis of the theory and practice of plane patterns, Washburn and Crowe (1988) have explained "how artworks reflect patterns of human behavior and basic values—both within one culture and among far-flung people." They have written the definitive guide in the use of affine geometry (Szabo 2002: 369) and flow-charting for the analysis of textile and decorative patterns from a symmetry point of view. In this article, we extend this repertoire of analytical tools by using other mathematical and statistical techniques, implemented in interactive pattern recognition software. At the same time, we contribute to the understanding of two different cultures through our study of the

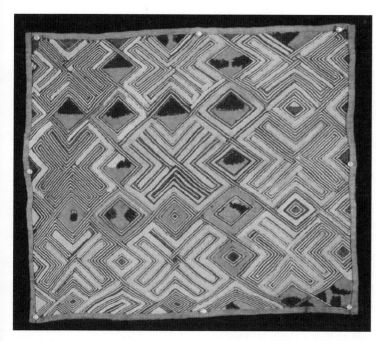

Figure 2
A typical West African Kuba cloth.

Figure 3
Canny edge detection applied to
Figure 2.

different geometric patterns that adorn their daily environments.

Digital Analysis of a Kuba Cloth Using Edge Detection

In order to identify appropriate digital tools for the analysis of the geometric content of Kuba cloths, the Concordia Center for Pattern Recognition and Machine Intelligence carried out a number of experiments to determine the suitability of different pattern recognition tools for the pattern analysis of such textiles. The mathematical techniques required for this work are documented in Gonzales (2002) and Canny (1986: 679). The original image is given in Figure 2. Our objective is to find intersecting lines in such figures.

Intuitively, an *edge* is a set of connected pixels that lie on the boundary between two regions. Edge detection is the most common method for locating meaningful discontinuities in gray levels. By edge detection, we can segment a given image and use the segments to identify the pattern of the image as a whole. We used and compared the results of several well-known image detection methods to study Figure 1: the Sobel operator, Prewitt operator, Robert operator, Laplacian operator, the Zero-crossing operator, and the Canny operator. We found that the Canny edge detection method, followed by an edge-merging process, gave the best result—a result that encodes a significant amount of useful information, subject to a tolerable level of noise. Figure 3 shows edges found using Canny algorithms on the cloth image in Figure 2.

Using a predefined threshold value, we merged "edge pixels" and were able to extract some of the geometric content of the given Kuba cloth, as illustrated in Figure 4.

Digital Analysis of a Zillij Mosaic Using Feature Extraction

It is clear from contemplating a number of Zillij mosaic images that they are composed of certain basic geometric objects such as stars, bullets, and hexagons. The challenge is to automate as much as possible the task of identifying these objects. A typical example of a Zillij mosaic is given in Figure 5.

In Zillij images, patterns are built up from a group of basic objects positioned using certain geometric rules of composition. An intuitive method is used first to identify the objects in a given image and group them into clusters using their geometric similarity. Each "cluster" then corresponds to a potential pattern. The next step is to find the rules of construction.

Extraction of the Basic Objects

The local binarization method (Niblack 1986: 115) turned out to be an effective method. By treating the basic objects as the "foreground" and the remaining components as the "background" of an image, we can use the binarization methods to extract objects from an image. In the case of Zillij mosaics, the local binarization method achieved better results than the global approach. Figure 6 shows the result of local binarization, applied to the image in Figure 5.

Feature Extraction

We begin by considering the *eccentricity* of an image. We do so by calculating for basic object its bounding ellipse (Szabo 2002: 530–3). The eccentricity of the object is defined as the ratio of the distance between the foci of the ellipse and the length of its major axis length.

Eccentricities are values between 0 and 1. The values 0 and 1 are degenerate cases. Ellipses whose eccentricities are 0 are actually circles, while ellipses whose eccentricities are 1 are line segments.

Next we calculate the *concavity* of the objects. For each pixel $p(x,y)$ on the contour, we get the two points $a(x_1, y_1)$ and $b(x_2, y_2)$ that are three dots ahead of and three dots behind p along the contour. We compute the midpoint between these points using the usual formula:

$$m((x_1+x_2)/2, (y_1+y_2)/2)$$

If *m* lies in the object, then the point *p* is convex, otherwise it is concave. The magnitude of the curvature is given by the Euclidean distance between *m* and *p*.

We then analyze the image further with the help of "Fourier descriptors" (Kauppinen 1995: 201). We find the *centroid* and the *contour* of each object. Finally, we calculate the distance between each point on the contour and the centroid. We use this information to convert a given two-dimensional object into a one-dimensional signal called the *curve signature* of the object. The discrete Fourier transform (Wolfram 1996: 868)

Figure 4
Merged edge pixels.

Figure 5
A Zillij mosaic.

Figure 6
Result of local binarization.

is then applied to each curve signature and the first ten terms in the Fourier series are used as the "feature" of the image.

Clustering

Next we create the *clusters*. We begin by using the eccentricity feature to divide the objects into two subgroups, one with a large eccentricity value and the other with a small eccentricity values. After some experimentation, the threshold was set to 0.65. For the subgroup of objects with large eccentricity value, we then divide the objects into two further subgroups based on the concavity feature: one without negative concavity value and one with negative concavity value. For each subgroup, a two-threshold sequential clustering scheme with refinement is used to cluster the objects into groups. For details, we refer to Theodoridis (1999). The final result is shown in Figure 7.

By comparing geometric details in Figures 5 and 7, we can see that the described method has potential as a user-guided digital tool for the geometric analysis of certain culturally significant patterns. Limitations include color fading and physical damage of a given pattern.

Digital Analysis of Artifacts Using Shape Grammars

Shape grammars have been of interest to us from the beginning of our research. Stiny and Gips pioneered this way of codifying design processes and requirements in the 1970s (Gips 1975; Stiny 1975), and their use has been promoted more recently by Terry W. Knight (1999). As computers become more powerful and allow faster and a more thorough analysis of patterns, allowing the allocations of more computing power to accommodating lay users, shape

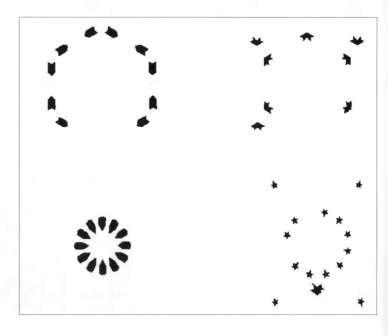

Figure 7
Some final groups.

grammars are poised to become practical computer-assisted design tools for a larger audience.

Shape grammars are designed to be easy for people to use. Shape grammars operate on the assumption that people are pretty good at picking out shapes from noisy backgrounds, ignoring scale and orientation, and judging acceptable matches between similar shapes. Computers tend to have problems with this and need domain-specific hints, limitations on input types, and idealizations of pattern to be able to execute, let alone extract, shape grammars. The extra effort of making the computer work in a somewhat awkward format brings us a process a little bit closer to how people approach designs—not as pixels, but as shapes—and is intended to return results that are usable by human designers and easily converted into digital design tools. We briefly describe some of the positive results achieved with the shape-grammar approach in the analysis of both Kuba cloths and Zillij mosaics.

Gips' and Stiny's papers were among the first to start with very simple patterns and recursively apply transformation rules to obtain more and more complex designs. They referred to these new systems as *shape grammar*. Tapia (1999) discusses a novel way of implementing such grammars. He proposes a visual technique that helps in the creation and application of shape grammars. Some researchers have also used shape-grammar techniques in other fields. For example, Dinesh Shikare's work (Shikare *et al.* 2001) on compression of three-dimensional objects is similar in spirit to the shape-grammar approach. Our method is an extension and generalization of these methods. While Gips and Tapia assume that basic patterns are given, we make no such assumption. Instead, we perform pattern analysis techniques on existing works of art to discover the basic patterns and hidden shape-grammar rules. We then provide visual tools to synthesize the new shape grammars from these basic patterns and rules.

For our purposes, a *pattern* A_n of order $n \geq 0$ is an arrangement of n line segments in space. We say a pattern A is *subpart* of another pattern B if all its line segments are also present in larger pattern. Two patterns A_n, B_n are said to be equivalent, $A_n \equiv B_n$ under transformation T if there exists some transformation T that transforms A to B. We think of equivalence classes of patterns as the metapatterns of our database. Transformations that are allowed generally depend on the domain of artwork being investigated. Sometimes full generality of linear transformations or even nonlinear transformation may be needed. In our case, the transformations that are allowed are scaling S, rotation R and translation T (Szabo 2002: 369).

A *rule* is a tool for generating new patterns from old ones. Thus a rule $U_{n,n+m}$ is an ordered pair (A_n, B_{n+m}) in the familiar sense of logic (Szabo 1978: 19). In our case, we restrict our attention to rules in which A is subpart of B, i.e. $A \subset B$.

A *shape grammar* is a set of rules $\{U_{n,n+m}^i\}, i \in N$ that gives us a way of generating new patterns from old ones, starting with given initial shapes (patterns).

In the present context, we are interested in grammars that allow us to represent and generate artifacts with optimal sets of initial patterns and plausible rules of construction.

Results

We sketch the ideas behind the algorithm that we devised for discovering shape grammars for Kuba cloths and Zillij mosaics. It consists of four distinct phases applied to a given artifact: preprocessing, recognition, replacement, and knowledge enhancement. Preprocessing is needed because many images have redundant and unnecessary information and small errors. We therefore transform the images into a format convenient for purposes. The recognition phase involves the discovery of recurring patterns in an artifact. Replacement involves the discovery of rules for transforming the discovered simple patterns into more complex ones. Knowledge enhancement, finally, completes the process and updates our database with new patterns and rules.

Preprocessing

For the discovery of patterns in the form of lines, triangles and similar shape grammars, it is easiest to deal with vector-based input. But available images can be either in raster format or in vector format. Hence a preprocessing step that takes raster images and converts them to vector-based format is required. At the same time, we want to remove unnecessary details in raster images and retain only essential features such as lines, edges, crossing, etc. For this purpose, we have written an interactive edge detection utility that provides many kinds of edge detection algorithms. Users can interactively change the parameters of the algorithms to achieve the best possible results, improving the performance of the detector by supplementing the algorithm with a human "oracle" while saving time over a completely manual trace. We also provide another utility to manually plot lines and edges, if necessary. This utility also converts the data format to *half-edge* data structures (see Gonzalez and Woods 2002).

Recognition

After preprocessing, we have the images in vector format. We use a half-edge data structure for storing and analyzing artifacts. Half-edge data structures can answer most queries. For example, they allow us to detect fairly quickly (in almost linear time) which edges are incidents of a given vertex. For each vertex we calculate its *feature vector*. As is clear from our earlier discussion, feature vectors consist of ordered sets of properties such as angles, length ratios, and so on. They provide us with information about which vertices are similar and therefore help us speed up the pattern identification process. Once we have an equivalence class of similar vertices, we traverse the neighborhoods of these vertices recursively. We repeat this process until the feature vectors match

within a prescribed tolerance. This process is know as "the growing of patterns." In our recent research, we have applied this process to recurring patterns discovered in Kuba cloths and Zillij mosaics with the use of neural networks (Wolfram Research 1999).

Replacement

During the growing phase of discovering patterns, we record both the original patterns and the grown pattern. This gives us a rule for transforming lower-order patterns into higher-order ones. If a pattern is selected by neural network, at least one chain of the lower-order patterns that led to this pattern is also selected. We sometimes shorten this process by giving rules that go directly from very simple patterns to more complex patterns in one step. In each case, we choose rules that give us the best description of a given pattern as a whole. At this point, we have only partial results in the identification of efficient construction rules for the shape grammars.

Knowledge Enhancement

Once we have the patterns and rules for a given artwork, we update the MetaPattern database with this new information. As we discover new patterns through our analysis of artifacts, we expand the growth phase of patterns by including the newly found patterns in the initial repertoire. The same holds true for rules. This means that as our database grows, so will our capacity for generating new works of art.

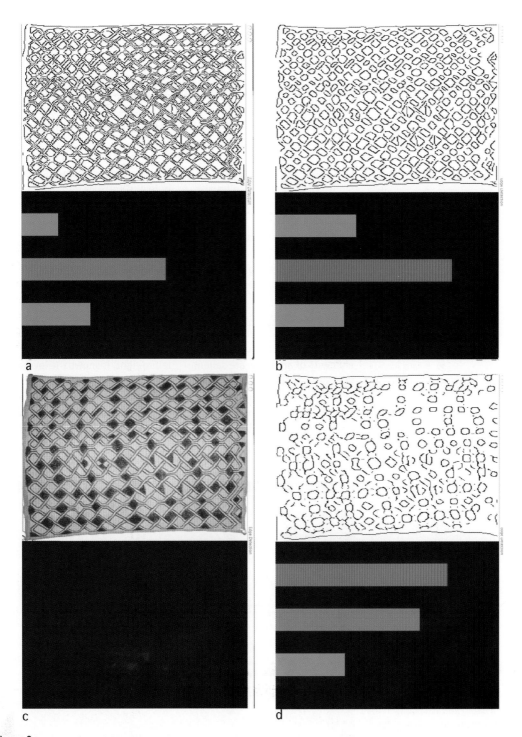

Figure 8
Edge detection using the Canny algorithm—various levels of detail: (a) low smoothing and low threshold for starting a line, (b) medium detail with balanced parameters, (c) original image with no edge detection, (d) with high smoothing applied.

Examples

Figure 8 shows a snapshot of the automatic edge detector in action. The three bars below each traced image indicate the values of the parameters of the algorithm used for edge detection. The first bar indicates the level of smoothing in preprocessing, the second sets a minimum "luminosity slope" threshold to start tracing a line, and the third adjusts the sensitivity of the line trace once started. The values can be changed dynamically. It is important to note that the edge detector actually displays the detection results in real time.

Figure 9 shows an alternative to automatic edge detection where the user can decide which elements of an image are salient features by using a manual edge-input program. This utility is a digital tool for creating vertices, edges, polygons. It also allows us to translate vertices and saves the result in a half-edge data structure.

It is clear from our discussion that edge detection as a tool for discovering the digital trace of an artifact is critical for the discovery of recurring geometric patterns in artifacts. From the results obtained it is clear that the shape-grammar approach to the geometric analysis of textile patterns and decorative design is more generally applicable than the separate methods for Kuba cloths and Zillij mosaics described earlier.

Figure 10 shows the output obtained by the recognition program. From the top down, the figure show different samples from Kuba, Zillij, and "other" categories found by the network. From left to right, it shows the levels of simplifications used before processing the images with neural networks—unprocessed, saturation maximized, resolution reduced and

Figure 9

An alternative to automatic edge detection: a manual input program where the user can click points in the design with the mouse and see the their numerical representation in the blue pane at the right. The gray box shows a close-up of the most recently added pair of lines.

Figure 10

Kuba, Zillij, and "other" patterns classified by a neural network.

linear transformation applied to color values of each pixel.

Classification of Artifacts Using Neural Networks

We conclude this article by discussing in greater depth the neural networks have helped us discern between Kuba and Zillij in an automated way, not identify initial shapes and patterns.

Neural networks (Haykin 1998) are a group of computer techniques that can deal well with noisy, incomplete data. The feed-forward and radial basis function networks we have been using (Wolfram Research 1999) take image data and assign them with varying degrees of certainty to categories that they have been trained to discern. Up till now, our network is able to distinguish fairly reliably between color images of Kuba cloths and Zillij mosaics: working from a training group of 135 images and verifying on 78, we achieved accurate classifications upwards of 90% of the time. All patterns that the network fails to classify are assigned to a third category. In building and expanding our database, trained neural networks will be able to perform initial sorts and provide additional measures of similarity between groups of patterns for shape-grammar analysis and other purposes.

In the next steps of our research, neural networks will also be used as an aid to creating new patterns. By having real designers and arts students evaluate output from early iterations, and using their input as data for a neural network to sort possible grammars into "user-friendly" and "user-unfriendly" groups, we are hoping to create a system that shies away from producing trivial or difficult-to-use patterns.

As described in Haykin (1994),

a neural network is a parallel distributed processor that has a natural propensity for storing experiential knowledge and making it available for use. It resembles to the brain in two respects: Knowledge is acquired by the network through a learning process and connection strengths known as synaptic weights are used to store the knowledge.

Artificial neural networks are based on our understanding of the human brain. Basically artificial neural networks are collections of mathematical models that emulate properties of biological nervous systems and adaptive biological learning. They are composed of a large number of highly interconnected processing elements that are analogous to neurons and are tied together with weighted connections that are analogous to synapses. Starting with measured data from some known or unknown source, neural networks are trained to perform classification, estimation, simulation, and prediction of the underlying process generating the data. Hence, neural networks are digital tools designed to estimate relationships in data, essentially a mapping or a function.

Neural networks are systems based on pattern recognition and iterations. Most of the neural networks have a *training* phase where the neurons are adjusted to the database. A neural network

is trained with inputs and it generates either a formula or a mapping system such that additional input can be assigned to a known class. Neural networks are used in many fields such as computer science, engineering, biology, psychology, physics, and business. Our work represents a new use of this technology: the study of cloth and culture through the classification and analysis of textile and decorative patterns.

There are many kinds of neural networks. Their main classification is into supervised and unsupervised networks. As the name implies, a supervised network is supervised, in other words, the database contains, for each input, the associated output. Then in the training session the network tries to establish connections between the inputs that are associated with the same output and make the distinction between those that are matched in this way. Unsupervised networks are autonomous: in the training process they try to discover which input should have the same output and which should not. To this end, the networks may look for common properties among inputs and create links between each of them. In the language used earlier this means that the network will establish equivalence classes among inputs. These classes can then be used in the way described in the use of shape grammars. Once our system is rich enough to allow artists to use it for the creation of new designs, we will use neural networks as tool for measuring the extent to which a new artifact, based on a real artifact stored in our database, is in harmony with the patterns of human behavior and basic values expressed in the geometric shape and complexity of the initial objects.

Conclusion

The results of this research were obtained using a combination of tools and techniques from mathematics, computer science, and fine arts. They represent a confluence of ideas and insights contributed in collaborative research by undergraduate students in cooperative study programs in mathematics and statistics, master's and doctoral students in computer science, and specialists in mathematics, art, and computer science.

The next phase of our work will take two directions: the construction of an interactive database of existing artifacts as a visual resource for the scientific and artistic communities, and the development of user-friendly digital tools for the study of these and other resources. The system will also provide additional tools for the generation of new works of art, based on the models in the database. We envisage these activities as culminating in the creation of a "visual studio" for the artistic, cultural, and scientific exploration of geometry-based objects of our human heritage, expressed through regional cultures.

Acknowledgments

Drs Kolak Dudek, Sharman, and Szabo gratefully acknowledge the support for this research by the Fonds québécois de la recherche sur la société et la culture. We also acknowledge with thanks the contributions of Yun Li and Wumo Pan of the Center for Pattern Recognition and Machine Intelligence of Concordia University to the extraction problem, and that of Mélanie Béchard, a Concordia University cooperative education undergraduate in pure and applied mathematics, to the classification problem.

Notes

1. This reference is specific to catalog item no. 74 in the exhibition catalog *Treasures from the Bronze Age of China: An Exhibition from the People's Republic of China*, The Metropolitan Museum of Art, 1980. Item no. 74 was on loan from the Hunan Provincial Museum. Many other vessels, bells, and objects in the exhibition were also inscribed with figurative geometric abstractions, i.e. dragon motifs common to early Chinese bronze, including vessels from the Shang culture (fifteenth–fourteenth century BC).

2. Jorge Enciso (1971), Custodian of Colonial Monuments and Assistant Director of the National Institute of Anthropology and History in Mexico City in the 1920s, documented the inscriptions on malacates, spindle whorls found in archaeological digs. Many of the circular images are decorated with geometric abstractions (pp. 80–5, Xicalcoliuhqui fret), but just as many others have geometric animal designs, particularly pp. 15–22. His drawings were reproduced in Enciso (1971).

References

Adams, Monni. 1973. "Kuba Embroidered Cloth." *African Art* 12(1): 24–39.

Arnett, William and Paul Arnett. 2002. *On the Map. The Quilts of Gee's Bend*. Atlanta, GA: Tinwood Books in association with the Museum of Fine Arts, Houston, TX.

Canny, John. 1986. "A Computational Approach to Edge Detection." *IEEE Transactions on Pattern Analysis and Machine Intelligence* 8(6): 679–98.

Courant, Richard and Herbert Robbins. 1941. *What Is Mathematics?* New York: Oxford University Press.

Critchlow, Keith. 1976. *Islamic Patterns: A Cosmological Approach*. London: Thames & Hudson.

Eglash, Ron. 1999. *African Fractals: Modern Computing and Indigenous Design*. New Brunswick, NJ: Rutgers University Press.

El-Said, Issam and Ayse Parman. 1976. *Geometric Concepts in Islamic Art*. London: Scorpion Publishing.

Enciso, Jorge. 1971. *Designs from Pre-Colombian Mexico*. New York: Dover.

Gips, James. 1975. *Shape Grammars and Their Uses: Artificial Perception, Shape Generation and Computer Aesthetics*. Basel and Stuttgart: Birkhäuser Verlag.

Gonzalez, Rafael C. and Richard E. Woods. 2002. *Digital Image Processing*, 2nd edn. Reading, MA: Addison-Wesley.

Haykin, Simon. 1998. *Neural Networks: A Comprehensive Foundation*, 2nd edn. Englewood Cliffs, NJ: Prentice Hall.

Haykin, Simon. 1994. *Neural Networks: A Comprehensive Foundation*. New York: Macmillan.

Hasimoto, Shuji. 2000. *Multimedia Modeling: Modeling Multimedia Information and Systems*. Tokyo: Waseda University.

Kauppinen, H., Tapio Seppänen and Matti Pietikäiner. 1995. "An Experimental Comparison of Autoregressive and Fourier-based Descriptors in 2D Shape Classification." IEEE *Transactions on Pattern Analysis and Machine Intelligence* 17(2): 201–7.

Knight, Terry W. 1999. *Shape Grammars*: Six Types. *Environment and Planning B: Planning and Design* 26: 15–31.

Kolak Dudek, Cheryl, Lydia Sharman and Fred E. Szabo. 2003. "Interactive Grammar Systems for Generative Design." *9th International Conference on Virtual Systems and Multimedia: Hybrid Reality (Art, Technology, and the Human Factor)*. Montreal, Quebec, pp. 129–35.

Livingston, Jane. 2002. *Reflections on the Art of Gee's Bend. The Quilts of Gee's Bend*. Atlanta, GA: Tinwood Books in association with the Museum of Fine Arts, Houston, TX.

Niblack, Wayne. 1986. *An Introduction to Digital Image Processing*. London: Prentice Hall.

Sharman, Lydia. 1994. *The Amazing Book of Shapes*. London: Dorling Kindersley.

Sharman, Lydia. 1996. *Teaching Maths through Islamic Art*, 2nd edn. London: Victoria and Albert Museum.

Shikhare, Dinesh, Sushil Bhakar and S. P. Mudur. 2001. "Compression of Large 3D Engineering Models Using Automatic Discovery of Repeating Geometric Features." *6th International Fall Workshop on Vision, Modeling and Visualization*, Stuttgart, Germany.

Stiny, George. 1975. *Pictorial and Formal Aspects of Shape and Shape Grammars: On Computer Generation of Aesthetic Objects*. Basel: Birkhäuser Verlag.

Szabo, Fred E. 1978. *Algebra of Proofs*. Amsterdam: North-Holland Publishing.

Szabo, Fred E. 2002. *Linear Algebra: An Introduction Using Maple*. Boston, MA: Harcourt Academic Press.

Tapia, M. 1999. "A Visual Implementation of a Shape Grammar System." *Environment and Planning B: Planning and Design* 26: 59–73.

Theodoridis, S. and K. Koutroumbas. 1999. *Pattern Recognition*. Boston, MA: Academic Press.

Washburn, Dorothy K. and Donald W. Crowe. 1988. *Symmetries of Culture: Theory and Practice of Plane Pattern Analysis*. Seattle, WA and London: University of Washington Press.

Wolfram, Stephen. 1996. *The Mathematica Book*, 3rd edn. Cambridge, MA: Cambridge University Press.

Wolfram Research. 1999. *Neural Networks*. Champaign, IL: Wolfram Research.

Further Reading

Gersho, Allen and Robert M. Gray. 1992. *Vector Quantization and Signal Compression*. Boston, MA: Kluwer Academic Publishers.

Gips, James and George Stiny. 1975. "An Investigation of Algorithmic Aesthetics." *Leonardo* 8(3): 213–20.

Grabar, Oleg. 1992. *The Mediation of Ornament*. Princeton, NJ: Princeton University Press.

Hassoun, M. H. 1995. *Fundamentals of Artificial Neural Networks*. Cambridge, MA: MIT Press.

Hedgecoe, John and Salma Samar Damluji. 1992. *Zillij, the Art of Moroccan Ceramics*. London, UK: Garnet Publishing.

Herz, J., A. Krough, and R.G. Palmer. 1991. *Introduction to the Theory of Neural Computation*. Reading, MA: Addison-Wesley.

Johansson, R. 1993. *System Modeling and Identification*. Englewood Cliffs, NJ: Prentice Hall.

Kirsch, Joan L. and Russell A. Kirsch. 1986. "The Anatomy of Painting Style: Description with Computer Rules." *Environment and Planning B: Planning and Design* 13: 163–76.

Knight, Terry W. 1993. "Color Grammars: The Representation of Form and Color in Designs." *Leonardo* 26(2): 117–24.

Knight, Terry W. 1994. *Transformations in Design*. Cambridge: Cambridge University Press.

Koza, John R. 1992. *Genetic Programming: On the Programming of Computers by Means of Natural Selection*, pp. 16–62. Cambridge, MA: MIT Press.

Ljung, L. and T. Glad. 1994. *Modeling of Dynamic Systems*. Englewood Cliffs, NJ: Prentice Hall.

March, L. 1996. "Rulebound Unruliness." *Environment and Planning B: Planning and Design* 23: 396–405.

March, L. 1999. "Architectonics of Proportion: A Shape Grammatical Depiction of Classical Theory." *Environment and Planning B: Planning and Design* 26: 91–100.

Meurant, Georges. 1986. *Shoowa Design*. London: Thames & Hudson.

Mitchell, Tom M. 1997. *Machine Learning*. New York: McGraw-Hill.

Necipoglu, Gulru. 1995. *The Topkapi Scroll: Geometry and Ornament in Islamic Architecture*. Santa Monica, CA: The Getty Center for the History of Art and the Humanities.

Stiny, George and James Gips. 1978. *Algorithmic Aesthetics: Computer Models for Criticism and Design in the Arts*. Los Angeles, CA: University of California Press.

Super *Cilia* Skin:
A Textural Interface

Abstract

The Tangible Media Group has done a series of investigations into new multi-modal computer interfaces that utilize gesture and the sense of touch to improve interpersonal communication, education, and access to digital information. "Interactive surfaces" are one of our most promising lines of research and this article will look in depth at the design, implementation, and possible applications of interactive surfaces through an example project, Super Cilia Skin, an Interactive Membrane.

Super Cilia Skin (SCS) is a computationally enhanced membrane that couples tactile/kinesthetic input with tactile and visual output. Our prototype manipulates the orientation of an array of yarn-like actuators (cilia) to display dynamic images or physical gestures. Like cloth, SCS is designed to be applied to arbitrary objects to engage sight and touch. Unlike traditional textiles, SCS can sense touch and dynamically move its surface. This article will discuss the potential for scale shifts with actuated textiles in which the material can blur boundaries between foreground/environment and field/object. Our design studies will present applications in which actuated textiles can use their material properties to improve interpersonal communication, enhance creative expression, and assist education in young learners by engaging tactile/kinesthetic intelligences.

HAYES RAFFLE, JAMES TICHENOR AND HIROSHI ISHII

Hayes Raffle is developing materials with memory and researching their applications to education and the arts. Before attending MIT, he studied sculpture at Yale College, founded Rafelandia Design, and codesigned the award-winning ZOOB® building toy.

James Tichenor is conducting research in Design and Computation at the MIT School of Architecture. His current investigations address issues of architectural surface with digitally manipulated materials. Before attending MIT, he worked for Konyk Architecture and cofounded FourPlus Design.

Hiroshi Ishii's research focuses upon the design of seamless interfaces between humans, digital information, and the physical environment. He is a tenured associate professor of Media Arts and Sciences, at the MIT Media Lab. To pursue his vision of "Tangible Bits," Professor Ishii founded the Tangible Media Group at the MIT Media Lab at the end of 1995.

Textile, Volume 2, Issue 3, pp. 328–347
Reprints available directly from the Publishers.
Photocopying permitted by licence only.
© 2004 Berg. Printed in the United Kingdom.

Super *Cilia* Skin: A Textural Interface

Introduction

For thousands of years people have sought to design environments, tools, and objects to define their context in the natural world. Man-made objects such as buildings and clothing are designed as boundaries between the body and the natural environment, whereas art objects are often created for emotional reflection or communication. The surge of computers in the last half-century has led to a variety of research that intends to find both meaning and context for a world filled with "intelligent" machines. Where some have created tools to improve human productivity, others have explored philosophical and aesthetic investigations through the creation of interactive art works and responsive environments.

The Tangible Media Group at the MIT Media Lab conducts research in "Tangible Interfaces" with a vision to improve people's access to computers by creating computational media that take advantage of existing skills people have developed through working with physical objects (Ishii and Ullmer 1997: 234). These platforms and digitally enhanced objects aim to bridge the intangible world of digital information with the physical world.

As part of our ongoing research we developed a prototype textural interface called Super Cilia Skin (SCS; Figure 1). SCS is an interactive membrane designed by Hayes Raffle, James Tichenor, and Mitchell Joachim that allows two people to communicate over a distance by manipulating the orientations of an array of yarn-like actuators (Raffle 2003: 529). SCS metaphorically interprets biological "skin" as an actuated, sensory interface between a computer and its environment. Skin is protective, sensory and tactile, touch being our only sense capable of both sensing and manipulating the environment. Applying this metaphor across multiple scales allows one to imagine a skin that can clothe small objects, the body, or the environment. This is similar to traditional textiles, in which material can transcend scale to engage people, touch, material, and environment, the difference being that a digital textural

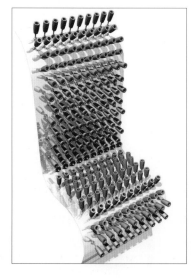

Figure 1
SCS conceptual rendering.
Photo: Mitchell Joachim,
© 2002 Mitchell Joachim.

interface provides a gateway to information technology.

In this article, we consider the many opportunities afforded by an interactive membrane and address how a tactile material could both represent and provide the ability to create information. Reflecting upon our experiences designing and testing our prototype, we will discuss possibilities with actuated textiles as a benefit to children's learning, interpersonal communication, and architectural design. Since we created SCS to be a material available to designers, this article will begin with an overview of the development of our prototype and will then explore potential applications for actuated textiles by drawing on examples from various fields of study.

Figure 2

Images of wind blowing over grassy fields inspired SCS. Photo: Hayes Raffle, © 2003 Hayes Raffle.

SCS

SCS is a tactile and visual system inspired by the beauty of grass blowing in the wind (Figures 2 and 3). It is made of an elastic membrane covered with an array of felt actuators (cilia). These cilia move in response to computer-controlled magnetic fields created under the membrane, allowing them to represent information by dynamically changing their physical orientation (see Figure 12). The device is designed to sense physical gestures on the cilia and to replay those gestures by wiggling the same cilia that were touched. Because SCS converts gesture to computer data, multiple Super Cilia Skin devices may communicate over a distance using a standard computer network. For example, where a telephone allows

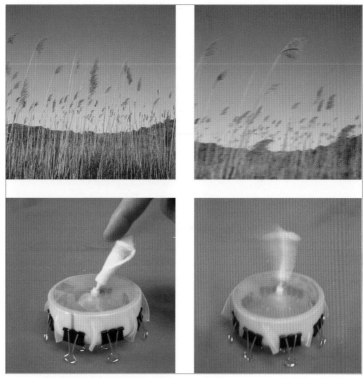

Figure 3

The movements of grass are re-created with felt actuators in an elastic membrane. Photo: Hayes Raffle, © 2004 Hayes Raffle.

two people to talk to each other over a distance, two SCS devices may be used to communicate remote gesture (Brave *et al.* 1998: 169). Similarly, the system can be used alone to display previously recorded information.

While our current prototype functions only on a table top, our studies suggest that creating a scalable, tactilely expressive fabric may be possible. This fabric would record and playback physical gestures on its surface or synchronize motions across two paired objects to support intimate physical communication.

Design Process

The development of SCS was guided more by aesthetic decisions chosen for their appeal to us as artists and designers, than by engineering decisions chosen to create an optimized performance. This approach contextualizes a type of research that focuses on the history and chronology of craft. The craft tradition embodies a history of people who have a knowledge of how things are made and how to make things with which people intimately interact. This was an important foundation for our development of SCS because computer technology has traditionally been developed either as engineering with a clear solution, or as art whose value cannot be easily measured.

In the design of SCS we built upon existing tangible interface research and used the concept of scale to expand this work in new ways. In the history of tangible interfaces, materials are rather rare. While "Tangible Bits" described a vision for interactive

surfaces (Ishii and Ullmer 1997: 234), most tangible interfaces have been presented as tools or design objects with specific purposes. From its conception, SCS was intended to be a scalable, multi-modal material that could transmit meaning through tactile and visual movement.

The term *cilia* refers to microorganisms such as paramecium that use small hair-like structures—cilia—for locomotion. By moving these cilia in rhythm, these animals are able to move through fluid, not unlike a boat with many people rowing. There has been research in the MEMS community to use microscopic man-made cilia for locomotion (Suh *et al.* 2000: 1101). Changing the scale of the cilia to that of the hand or body changes the cilia's function and the ways that people can interact with them.

Many metaphors for macro-scale cilia fill our environments. Wind-swept grass, vacuum-cleaner tracks on shag carpet, mowed baseball fields, and kinetic sculptures all influenced our understanding of the concept of a textural field. Many of these cilia oscillate with different mechanisms. For instance, the San Francisco Exploratorium presents a gravity-powered field of undulating pendulums that oscillate in response to one's touch (Fleming 1980). The top surface of these oscillating pins describes movement across a horizontal plane. This oscillatory mechanism is fundamentally different than microscopic sensory hairs in our ears that convert air movements into hearing. These hairs are anchored in the tympanic membrane of our ear canals, and their static orientations are maintained by the elasticity of the membrane. This mechanism inspired an elastic membrane for SCS, in which macro-scale cilia can cover curved surfaces and have consistent behaviors independently of gravity.

Design Evolution

Looking to examples of textural metaphors in our environments, we tested a variety of materials for prototype cilia, including yarn, cotton batting, wool rope, wire chenille, natural twigs and leaves, pom-poms, and bottle brushes (Figures 4 and 5). Our earliest prototype used cotton swabs anchored in a highly plasticized vinyl membrane (Figures 6, 7 and 8). By gluing small magnets to the bases of these swabs, we found we could easily control their general orientations with a separate magnet. The softness of the swabs encouraged people to put the prototype next to their faces, describing the sensation as similar to the "butterfly kiss" created when someone transmits a gesture with one's eyelashes.

Magnetic fields allowed us easily to create force fields on the cilia that dispersed with distance in a manner similar to wind (Figure 9). The Actuated Workbench (Figure 10) allows a computer to "draw" with magnetic fields (Pangaro *et al.* 2002: 181), and our prototypes employed various densities of cilia that converted these magnetic fields into mechanical movement (Figures 11 and 12).

Our early design studies explored density and aspect

Figures 4 and 5
Wool yarn inspired the tactile and visual qualities of our prototype cilia. Photo: Hayes Raffle, © 2002 Hayes Raffle.

ratio of the cilia and their tactile responses when anchored in various kinds of membranes. Looking to existing examples of textures and natural fields, we found consistent relationships between field and object: a forest, like a tree or a shrub, appears as both surface and structure when viewed at different distances. From an airplane, one notices the surface of the forest canopy. However, as one descends towards the individual trees one notices that tree trunks bifurcate into branches and branches divide into twigs to end with leaves. The change from field to object is an abrupt perceptual shift.

We compared these visual perceptual changes to our tactile perception of material texture. By

Figures 6, 7, and 8
Prototypes tested different materials, cilia densities, and aspect ratios. These used cotton swabs and plasticized vinyl. Photos: Mitchell Joachim, © 2002 Mitchell Joachim.

creating both three-dimensional computer models and physical models (Figures 13 and 14), we were able to quickly test different shapes and scales of cilia to establish an aesthetically satisfying balance between surface and texture. Since our prototype was designed to be manipulated by people's hands,

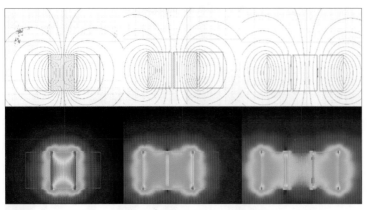

Figure 11
SCS Prototype on top of the Actuated
Workbench. Photo: Hayes Raffle,
© 2004 MIT Media Lab.

Figure 9
The interactions of the magnetic fields of Actuated Workbench combine and
disperse with distance replicating the interactions of wind across a field.
Photo: Gian Pangaro, © 2002 MIT Media Lab.

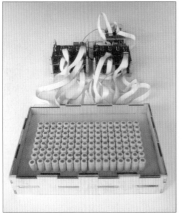

Figure 10
The Actuated Workbench. Photo:
Hayes Raffle, © 2004 MIT Media Lab.

Figure 12
SCS prototype "draws" with magnetic
fields. Photo: Hayes Raffle, © 2004
MIT Media Lab.

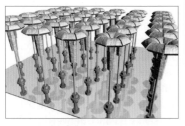

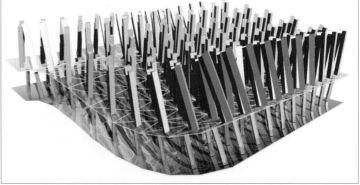

Figures 13 and 14
Various 3D renderings addressed issues of scale, relationships to natural forms and mechanical stability. Photo:
Mitchell Joachim, © 2002 Mitchell Joachim.

we chose to make our prototype's cilia slightly smaller than our fingers and to space them with about 50% density. This gave the material a familiar "feel," as well as a perceptual balance between surface, volume, and tactile depth.

History of Physical Displays

While actuated displays are a traditional focus of research in the haptics community (Wagner *et al.* 2002), SCS was inspired by artistic and architectural investigations into kinetic surfaces. A recent surge in kinetic sculpture and computer-controlled installation has allowed a variety of artists and designers to use form to depict dynamic change in novel and surprising ways. For instance, architect and kinetic sculptor Tim Prentice uses wind as a driving mechanism for "Wind Frame," a grid of galvanized steel panels that oscillate in the wind (Figure 15). These panels variably reflect the sky and ground towards the viewer, revealing the waves of wind around the viewer. Tactile wind and visual sky converge in the Wind Frame with a mechanism at once simple and sophisticated.

In a similar vein, sculptor Danny Rozin created "Wooden Mirror," a technologically driven array of wooden blocks that change orientation to create a pictorial "reflection" of the viewer of the piece (Figure 16). Wooden Mirror

Figures 15
Tim Prentice's Square Wind Frame converts wind into fluctuating reflections of the earth and sky. Photo: Tim Prentice, © 1980 Tim Prentice.

Figures 16
Danny Rozin's Wooden Mirror uses live video data and servo motors to reflect the viewer and his environment in an array of motorized wooden blocks. Photo: Daniel Rozin, © 2000 Daniel Rozin.

points a video camera at the viewer and drives many small motors to angle carefully the array of wooden blocks, controlling the depth of shadows on the surfaces of the blocks. Where Prentice's Wind Frame is a formal and visual translation of natural phenomena, Wooden Mirror is more a translation of digital phenomena: Rozin has turned humble wooden blocks into "pixels" that can create a reflection of almost anything digital.

Rozin's mirror is built at a figurative scale, framing the body and its environs. An architectural extension of an actuated mosaic was explored by Goldthorpe with the "Aegis Hyposurface," a sculptural investigation into visual representation and kinetic architecture (Burry 2003: 18). While the Hyposurface has a skin similar to Prentice's Wind Frame, it draws its energy from a grid of pneumatic pistons behind its reflective steel scrim. Due to its construction, the Hyposurface naturally creates wave-like undulations when its pistons "draw." In addition to being a visual display, it is a physical and aural intrusion into a space, an active wall that temporally protrudes into the room that it helps to define. While its drawings are not triggered by immediate environmental stimuli, Aegis Hyposurface exhibits the potential impact of actuated skins built at a tectonic scale.

SCS builds on this history of kinetic displays and adds the element of tactile input, transforming the kinetic display into a tangible interface. This shifts material from a role of strict representation to a means to project human intention into the machine. Material can therefore facilitate a form of gestural "programming" that opens up surprising design possibilities.

Kinesthesia and Education (Touch and Toys)

A potential value of tangible information interfaces is their connection to our bodies, our senses of touch and kinesthesia (Figure 17). As well as being aesthetically engaging, physical experiences have important roles in learning. Toys and educational tools helped inspire the design of SCS, and we believe that actuated textural interfaces could add beneficial qualities to existing educational tools and support existing educational practices.

The potential for textiles and texture to support children's learning is evident when one looks around a typical American infant/toddler nursery. Colors and textures abound, from textured foam books to teething objects to plush teddy bears and other

Figure 17
SCS adds a skin-like sense of touch to a visual material creating a tangible interface to computational information. Photo: Hayes Raffle, © 2004 Hayes Raffle.

stuffed toys. In the design of young children's toys, great care is given to the tactile qualities of materials. As we researched familiar instances of textures in our daily lives to develop SCS, we found the highest number and most distinct "textural signatures" among children's toys.

The prevalence of texture in children's artifacts can be traced back to the cognitive, social, and educative roles that physical interactivity with objects holds for children. Movement occupies a central position in human activity (Laban 1975 [1956]) and it is a central feature of early learning (Piaget 1952). Recent studies in children's education have argued that children have a separate bodily intelligence that includes masterful coordination of their body movements and the ability to manipulate objects in a skilled manner (Gardner 1983). Bodily kinesthetic intelligence may, in fact, be central to academic learning (Seitz 1992: 35).

Frederick Froebel's Kindergarten provides an early and important instance of specialized objects in education. Froebel distilled his worldview into a number of kindergarten "gifts," physical objects that children used in daily lessons to learn about common forms and processes found in nature. The kindergarten gifts had a deep influence on twentieth-century art. For instance, Frank Lloyd Wright credited kindergarten as the basis for his aesthetic vocabulary, and many of his architectural forms are similar to artifacts from the kindergarten classroom (Brosterman 1997: 138). Such evidence shows the strong influence educational objects can have on children's aesthetic development.

Physical materials can also help children develop skills manipulating abstract concepts. Educational manipulatives are toys that are specially designed to help children with this. For example, "Cuisinaire rods" allow children to explore the abstract concepts of arithmetic by manipulating physical blocks of different lengths. By arranging blocks to create series of equal length, children can discover that $1+3=2+2$.

While the use of physical materials in education has a rich history in the last century (Brosterman 1997: 21), the introduction of computers to classrooms has focused on screen-based activities. In an effort to develop an alternative to screen-based computer activities, Mitchel Resnick presented "Digital Manipulatives," arguing that interactive, programmable materials can take advantage of the privileged role of physical, tactile material in children's education while using computers to make certain complex ideas accessible to them (Resnick *et al.* 1998: 281). Where wooden blocks allow kids to make towers that fall over and thus understand static structures and gravity, programmable blocks may allow kids to understand concepts like feedback and emergence in closed systems, concepts that are not usually taught until college age. Computers, coupled with physical manipulatives, may therefore help children to understand ideas that educators previously considered too complex for them (Resnick *et al.* 1998: 287).

One outcome of this work is the development of computer interfaces that are programmed through physical interaction, and some of these projects have explored the idea that material can have memory. For example, "Topobo" is a building toy with kinetic memory that can help children aged seven and older to learn about dynamic balance (Figure 18). Topobo is akin to building systems like LEGO® or ZOOB® that kids can use to make imaginative creations. The difference is that Topobo has motorized parts that can repeat the motions a child has made to them. To use Topobo, a child may snap together parts to create a fanciful animal, teach their animal how to walk by physically manipulating its bodily movements, and then observe the animal walk on its own. Topobo allows children aged 7–13 to experiment with concepts like dynamic balance and system coordination (Raffle *et al.* 2004: 875). Topobo is a scalable, modular, actuated system with which other people design objects, and thus shares conceptual "material qualities" with SCS.

A textural information interface may allow children to explore certain abstract concepts through physical manipulation of a material. Interaction with a teddy bear is typically physical interaction with the bear's material properties; bears that are soft, squishy, and textural are often chosen for those qualities. A natural design evolution is to use those same material qualities to interact with a "smart" teddy bear.

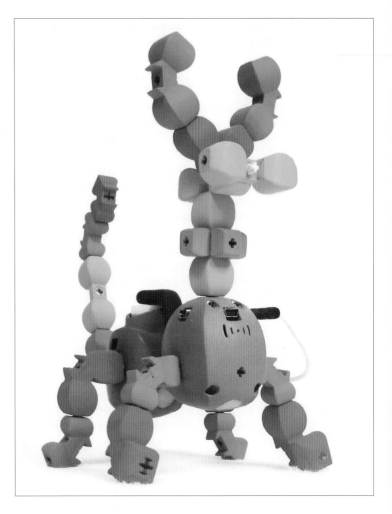

Figure 18
The Topobo building toy with "kinetic memory" that allows children to sculpt with form and motion. Topobo is a scalable, modular, actuated system with which other people design objects, and thus shares conceptual "material qualities" with SCS. Photo: Hayes Raffle, © 2003 Hayes Raffle.

One might imagine a teddy bear clothed in SCS (Figures 19 and 20) that has textural memory, and can replay a child's gesture on its body with a sort of physical "echo" or reflection of the child's motion. When a child rubs the bear, it can later mimic the movement of its fur, acknowledging to the child that the child rubbed it. Through repetition, the child may embody specific gestures with meaning and emotion. For instance, if the child rubs the bear's stomach every time he hugs it, the bear might learn to wiggle its own tummy when it "wants" a hug. Integrating computation into soft stuffed toys, which are both tangible and part of the child's early environment, can support a more familiar, less intimidating, and more emotionally engaging atmosphere for children than other types of computerized interfaces (Cassell and Ryokai 2001: 209).

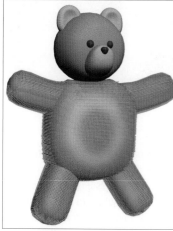

Figures 19 and 20
SCS could someday be wrapped around children's toys to engage emotions and support learning. Photos and ©: © 2002 Mitchell Joachim, © 2004 James Tichenor.

Digital textiles could also enable cloth to assume the role of display and interface in interactive toys, allowing plush toys to be "interactive" without today's typical flashing lights and recorded voice clips that line toy-store aisles. For example, a plush teddy bear covered with SCS might wiggle its ears and draw a circle on its tummy in response to a child's careful attention. The bear could use cilia movements and sound to convey excitement or happiness in response to a toddler. Different behaviors from the child could elicit different tactile and audible responses from the teddy bear, encouraging the child to care for the bear. The value of such stimulus/response models in toys is evident in the success of products such as Furby™. However, toys like Furby often have limited physical interactions (e.g. vibrating), constraining the depth to which they can use tactile interactions to engage a child's emotions and encourage learning. Combining more sophisticated stimulus/response models with a tactile/kinesthetic interactive material like SCS could facilitate more educational computational toys that are truly "things-to-think-with" (Resnick *et al.* 1998: 282).

While SCS is not yet a thin, flexible, and affordable fabric that toy designers could wrap around a child's plush bear, computational textiles are advancing quickly and SCS offers an opportunity to consider how interactive textiles can support children's growth and learning. On one hand, there is a need to bridge digital interactivity with physical educational manipulatives. Textural interfaces can engage children's bodily-kinesthetic intelligences in interactive experiences, allowing children's physical engagement with material to reinforce cognitive development and learning experiences. On another hand, toys that flash lights and sound sirens to delight a child's senses are increasingly filling toy-store aisles. Such toys are certainly "sensory," but an actuated textile can facilitate a more organic, subtle, and creature-like interface than a siren or flashing light. It may be these subtle, organic qualities of textural materials that help children form the personal, emotional connections that make objects an important part of development.

Touch, Material, and Communication

We developed SCS, in part, to investigate how the physical qualities of material could be used to improve remote interpersonal communication (Raffle *et al.* 2003: 529). Communication is fundamentally a multi-modal experience, and touch is an important aspect of human interpersonal communication. Whether a pat on the back, a handshake or an intimate hug, touch conveys meaning and emotion that most communication technology struggles to transmit.

The Tangible Media Group has developed several devices over the past decade that have explored the extent to which shared physical objects can use technology to make remote communication more emotionally intimate and expressive. An early project called inTouch creates the illusion that two people, separated by a distance, can physically interact with the same physical object (Brave *et al.* 1998; Chang *et al.* 2002). The two connected objects, each made of three wooden cylindrical rollers mounted on a base (Figure 21), are connected over the Internet. When one of the rollers is rotated, the corresponding roller on the remote object rotates in the same way.

Figure 21
inTouch allows two people who are
separated by a distance to "share"
a physical object. © 1998 MIT Media
Lab. Photo: © 1998 MIT Media Lab.

A person using inTouch does
not perceive a simulation of the
other person, but is aware of
the device itself. The richness of
the interaction comes from the
representation of movement as
mediated by the coupled objects.
This is interesting in that it places
great importance on the physical
design of the device (Brave *et al.*
1998: 172). inTouch demonstrated
that an abstract tactile interface
can allow a broad emotional range
of expression since the device
itself will not dictate a certain
interpretation of its movements.

Our prototype SCS design
described two picture-framed,
electronically coupled SCS devices
that could sit on a table top or
hang on a wall like a painting. For
instance, I might have one device
in my living room and my sister
may have a coupled device in
her living room. When we talk on

the phone I might draw gestures
on my device that she can see
and feel on hers (Figure 22). We
might collaborate to draw gestural
images, beat a musical rhythm
back and forth, or casually respond
to each others' movements of the
cilia (Chang *et al.* 2001: 313).

Figure 22
SCS uses texture to allow remote
interpersonal communication to
engage sight and touch. A gesture
can be seen, or an image can be
felt. Photo: Hayes Raffle,
© 2004 Hayes Raffle.

If the same device were built to respond to shadows, it could operate as an ambient information interface (Wisneski *et al.* 1998: 22). As I would occasionally see a representation of my sister's shadow as she walks by her device, I would become aware that she is home and active, and I may strike up an active dialogue between us. The subtle, abstract nature of the cilia is less invasive than pictorial representation like a video conference and invites our participation only when our peripheral awareness is engaged and we choose to open a human channel of communication.

A baby's crib blanket might trigger a small SCS in the parents' kitchen to mimic the baby's bodily gestures over the surface of her blanket. As she rolls around in her crib, a parent might notice if she is restless or peaceful, giving the parent a sense of her physical state. Where a common "baby monitor" can remotely tell you something about a child's speech, an actuated textile might tell a parent or loved one something about the baby's body language.

Placed in a working parent's office across town, the same device can hold a different meaning. Textural changes on the remote device allow an awareness of the child's presence and motion on her own blanket. As the parent occasionally notices that baby is in her crib, resting peacefully or rolling around with life, the parent may feel more closely connected to their child (Weinberg *et al.* 1998: 326). Since SCS is a bidirectional interface, we wonder if parents would want to remotely "touch" their child. That is, touching the

office display with one's fingers would cause subtle manipulations on the surface of the baby's blanket. This sort of physical telepresence may help the parent and child form stronger emotional connections despite their temporary physical separation.

SCS as a fabric on the back of cell phones allows a different kind of conversation. A typical phone call may interrupt an ongoing vocal conversation between the recipient of the call and a third person. The recipient may not want to answer the phone, however. He may reach in to his pocket and give the cilia a gentle back and forth gesture to signal to the caller, "not now." Such a gesture can happen without disrupting the flow of the ongoing conversation (Chang *et al.* 2002: 315; Figure 23).

Textural interfaces may facilitate more emotionally rich communication in the future. Designers could engage people's interpretation of texture and incorporate more of people's senses into technology-mediated communication, making the communication richer and more memorable. However, scale and context carry added meaning because bidirectional interfaces may or may not be identically designed and may or may not be in identical contextual settings. As we learned from inTouch, these design decisions will affect how communication is perceived and conducted. While this section focused on applications tailored to hand and finger gestures, other applications may address communication involving the whole body or environment.

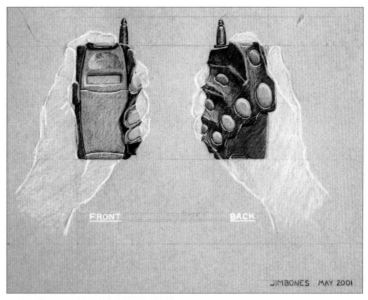

Figure 23
ComTouch introduced haptic communication to cell phones. SCS could also support tactile cell phone communication. Photo: © 2001 MIT Media Lab.

Architecture

Our design decision to make SCS a scalable material rather then an object supported our goal for the surface to be used on an architectural scale. As an interface changes its scale from object to environment, our perceptions and interactions with this interface change. This shift is analogous to the change from sculpture to architecture, and the development of various interactive surfaces invites a discussion of the changes in our spatial and peripheral understandings of an architectural scale interface.

In 1996 Kas Oosterhuis (1995) published the article "Liquid Architecture" describing the design of a pair of buildings known as the Salt-Water and Fresh-Water Pavilions, respectively designed by his firm Oosterhuis and the architectural firm Nox. These buildings incorporated numerous electronic sensors into their designs to gather information about both interior and exterior changes. This information ranged from the position of the visitors within the pavilions to the tidal flow of the neighboring sea. The incorporation of computer sensing and display technology in the design of the buildings was a touchstone in the architectural discourse of computationally enhanced environments in which the building is loosely defined as an interface. This concept builds upon age-old ideas that a building's envelope or "skin" mediates between a person and his or her environment. In a computationally enhanced environment, the surfaces are mediating not only between interior and exterior but also between the building's physical form and virtual information.

The architecture of the Salt-Water and Fresh-Water Pavilions, with their twisting amorphous forms, are exemplary of the digitally designed architecture of their time. The buildings' electronic interiors border on sensory overload, causing confusion between the tactile information of the buildings' forms and the projected virtual information. While this perceptual confusion can be seen as a goal of the designers, the opportunity to understand the presented virtual information is lost.

In the 1998 article "Ambient Displays: Turning Architectural Space into an Interface between People and Digital Information" (Wisneski *et al.* 1998) the Tangible Media Group helped forge the idea of ambient media as a research area within the field of human–computer interaction. The article discusses a number of ambient displays that use the background environment to give information to individuals. These displays range from pinwheels that spin at different rates depending upon the amount of change in a system to a projection of water ripples on a ceiling that represent the activity of distant relatives. The article also contextualizes the work within cognitive science research of foreground and background information processing.

The authors argue that one of the most effective uses of ambient displays is for "the display of information like natural phenomenon, such as atmospheric, astronomical, or geographical events"(Wisneski *et al.* 1998: 30). This is remarkably similar to the information that Nox and Oosterhuis chose to display in the interior of their pavilions with differing results. The restraint and specificity of the work of the Tangible Media Group contrasts sharply with the wild exuberance seen in the architectural designs of Kas Oosterhuis and his contemporaries. The ambient displays from the Tangible Media Group (and in much of the work of the human–computer interaction community) are informed by an engineering approach, that is with a clear set of goals and constraints. And thus many of the ambient displays do not seem integrated into the design of the environment, but remain as objects or projections onto it.

A digitally enhanced material such as SCS suggests solutions to problems within both of these approaches. As a surfacing material rather than an object or projection, SCS becomes an integral part of an environment. Incorporated into the design of its environment, it creates an experience where information can move seamlessly from background to foreground. By thinking of SCS as a surfacing material rather than as a display, we can draw from the rich history of interior surface design.

SCS could capitalize on traditional techniques of wallpaper design that mediate the difference between foreground and background information. That is, when we view wallpaper with a complex, repeating pattern, at some moments we tend to view the wallpaper as a field of background information, while at other times we focus on individual details with the foreground of our perception. In the same way, SCS as an interior wall surface could display fields of information that would be perceived either as background or as more detailed foreground information. Its main perceptual distinction (compared to wallpaper) would be its dynamic qualities. Decorative art such as wallpaper is not designed to be the single focus of attention: "[with] a painting," (or video screen, or projection), "even if we fail to see what the exact information on the picture or display is, we are aware that it is meant to be read as such" (Gombrich 1979: 116). The dynamic abilities of SCS would create sufficiently abstract "images" that, unlike a television or projection, the information could move to the background of our perception.

The interplay between foreground and ambient attention can be compared to a balance between pattern and image in which the visual imagery oscillates between representation and pure form. This oscillation is analogous to the confusion between the virtual and physical in the Salt-Water and Fresh-Water Pavilions. The use of pattern and repetition allows multiple readings (or layers of information) to exist at different scales. "Redundancy tends to drain individual elements of much of its meaning and character" (Gombrich 1979: 150), allowing differing patterns or elements within a field to form the focus of attention.

SCS naturally creates a static field of pattern with its repeating array of cilia. A grouping of cilia on SCS can carry semi-detailed information by dynamically generating a unit of pattern across its surface. These units create readings of both the surface itself (that is, the space), and of a more ambient reading of information. "Image" or foreground information then arises from disruptions or disturbances to this repeated pattern that are formed by contrasting movements or even static cilia. Where visual information in the Salt-Water and Fresh-Water pavilions was so overwhelming that it was perceived as texture rather than information, layering information within an intentional pattern could convey large-scale information as multiple layers of meaning that do not overwhelm the viewer.

Interior Design

The visual texture of tracks of a vacuum cleaner across shag carpet resonated as an early concept for SCS. As a medium of interaction, the floor plane is enticing because it is spatially connected to maps and human activity, and the floor registers regular tactile input from people's movement.

As a carpet, SCS might record or replay footsteps over its surface (Figure 24). Like inTouch, one could imagine two linked floors allowing an inhabitant to see the movement of people on the remote floor miles away. Such a carpet redefines the architecture around it as conflicted rooms become tactilely linked: mismatched floor plans would be revealed as ghostly footprints walk across the floor and disappear into a wall as a record of remote passers-by walking across a larger space.

Figure 24
An SCS carpet could display
remote footsteps in a friend's room.
Alternately, SCS could produce a live
weather map of wind over the US;
lying on the floor, the motion of the
jet stream would gain new meaning
as the turbulent wind gives a calming
massage. Photo: James Tichenor,
© 2004 James Tichenor.

SCS in a public space could compress time and, in a matter of minutes, replay days or months of people's movements. Patterns of ebb and flow would appear as the surface creates a full-scale visual and tactile experience (*Koyaanisqatsi* 1982).

Presenting large-scale dynamic phenomena such as the weather pattern of the United States, SCS reduces the scale of motion from kilometers to millimeters. As an information display, forecasts could be communicated in a subtle and continuous manner. While lying on the floor, the motion of the jet stream would gain new meaning as the turbulent wind gives a calming massage.

Exterior Facade
While investigating sensing methods with our prototype, we

found that movements of the cilia generate electrical power in the Actuated Workbench. Although we were investigating sensing techniques, we realized we could store this power for later use. We imagined SCS as an exterior skin on skyscrapers that could both visualize information as a billboard size display and harness energy of the wind forces that blow over the building's facade (Figure 25).

The idea that an alternative energy source can be a visually engaging material rather than a highly engineered object could increase the market for alternative energy. Rather than relying on a moralistic desire to tread less heavily on the earth, an SCS alternative energy facade would also be appealing for its strong visual character. The facade would take wind energy

Figure 25
SCS is imagined as an exterior
sheathing for skyscrapers that can
harness urban wind energy or
display billboard-size imagery.
Photo: James Tichenor,
© 2004 James Tichenor.

as its input and use pictorial
output to reflect current fashions
or display advertising. This
model challenges the traditional
function of a building's skin as a
barrier to protect people from the
forces of their environment, and
presents the architectural skin as
a membrane that can transform
the forces of nature into the energy
required to support the building's
inhabitants and the artificial nature
of its interior.

As provocative as these ideas
may be, further investigation
showed that they are not viable
with our current prototype.
But continuing research and
development may allow for
a surface that can harness
the physical motions of the
environment, turning the building
into an active part of its ecosystem.

Conclusion

Scale shifts from microscopic
biological cilia to body-scale cilia
informed our conception for SCS,
and we have imagined the material
at multiple scales to explore the
many possibilities that may be
afforded by actuated textiles. Our
prototype development was both
rewarding and humbling; reflecting
upon the aesthetic possibilities
and technical opportunities of our
models has allowed us to explore
more fully applications for tactile
surfaces. However, much more
work remains to be done. While
our current prototype functions
well as a planar display, curved
surfaces are currently difficult
to cover. We are investigating
a different approach in which

individual "hair follicles" could be inserted onto a curved surface (such as a teddy bear) like pins in a pincushion. Such investigations raise new technical and aesthetic considerations.

The development of electronic skins and fabrics is proceeding quickly, and a textural interface may be achievable in the near future. We believe that previous work in tangible interfaces, architectural design and interior surface design implies important application domains for interactive textiles, including intimate communication, children's education and aesthetically engaging interactive environments.

Throughout our design processes we have referred to the rich history of textile and surface design to guide our conceptual applications for SCS. Unlike other display technologies, textiles have the capacity to engage both sight and touch to convey information. In the future, they may also be able to engage these senses to collect information. We suspect that the absence of interesting textures in many of today's technological devices may be due to the absence of a textural interface. We look forward to a future in which designers can literally weave interactivity into the fabric of our environments.

Filmography
Koyaanisqatsi. 1982. Directed and written by Godfrey Reggio.

References

Brave, S., H. Ishii and A. Dahley. 1998. "Tangible Interfaces for Remote Collaboration and Communication," *Proceedings of CSCW '98*, 169–78. New York: ACM Press.

Brosterman, N. 1997. *Inventing Kindergarten*. New York: Harry N. Adams, Inc.

Burry, M. 2003. "Between Surface and Substance." *Architectural Design* 73(2) Mar/Apr: 8–20.

Cassell, J. and K. Ryokai. 2001. "Making Space for Voice: Technologies to Support Children's Fantasy and Storytelling." *Personal Technologies* 5(3): 203–24.

Chang, A., B. Resner, B. Koerner, X. Wang and H. Ishii. 2001. "LumiTouch: An Emotional Communication Device," *Extended Abstracts of Conference on Human Factors in Computing Systems (CHI '01)*, pp. 313–14. New York: ACM Press.

Chang, A., S. O'Modhrain, Jacob R. Gunther, E. Gunther and H. Ishii. 2002. "ComTouch: Design of a Vibrotactile Communication Device." *Proceedings of Design of Interactive Systems '02*, pp. 312–20. New York: ACM Press.

Fleming, W. Pinscreen. 1980. "San Francisco Exploratorium." http://www.exploratorium.edu/xref/exhibits/pinscreen.html.

Gardner, H. 1983. *Frames of Mind: The Theory of Multiple Intelligences*. New York: Basic Books.

Gombrich, E. H. 1979. *The Sense of Order: A Study in the Psychology of Decorative Art*. Ithaca, NY: Cornell University Press.

Ishii, H. and B. Ullmer. 1997. "Tangible Bits: Towards Seamless Interfaces between People,

Bits and Atoms." *Proceeding of Conference on Human Factors in Computing Systems (CHI) '97*, pp. 234–41. New York: ACM Press.

Laban, R. 1975 [1956]. *Principles of Dance and Movement Notation*, 2nd edn. Boston, MA: Plays.

Oosterhuis, Kas. 1995. "Liquid Architecture." *Archis* :11. Amsterdam: Stichting Artimo.

Pangaro, G., D. Maynes-Aminzade and H. Ishii. 2002. "The Actuated Workbench: Computer-controlled Actuation in Tabletop Tangible Interfaces." *Proceedings of Symposium on User Interface Software and Technology (UIST) '02*, pp. 181–90. New York: ACM Press.

Piaget, Jean. 1952. *The Origins of Intelligence in Children*, 2nd edn. Trans. M. Cook. New York: International Universities Press.

Raffle, H., J. Tichenor and M. Joachim. 2003. "Super *Cilia* Skin: an Interactive Membrane." *Extended proceedings on Human Factors in Computing Systems (CHI)*

'03, pp. 529–30. New York: ACM Press.

Raffle, H., A. Parkes and H. Ishii. 2004. "Topobo: A Constructive Assembly System with Kinetic Memory." *Proceedings on Human Factors in Computing Systems (CHI) '04*, pp. 869–77. New York: ACM Press.

Resnick, M., F. Martin, R. Berg, R. Borovoy, V. Colella, K. Kramer and B. Silverman. 1998. "Digital Manipulatives: New Toys to Think With." *Proceedings on Human Factors in Computing Systems*, pp. 281–7. New York: ACM Press.

Seitz, J. A. 1992. "The Development of Bodily-kinesthetic Intelligence in Children: Implications for Education and Artistry." *Holistic Education Review*, 35–9. Brandon, VT: Holistic Education Press.

Suh, J. W., R. B. Darling, K. F. Böhringer, B. R. Donald, H. Baltes and G. T. Kovacs. 2000. "Fully Programmable MEMS Ciliary Actuator Arrays for Micromanipulation Tasks." *IEEE*

International Conference on Robotics and Automation (ICRA) '02, pp. 1101–8. San Francisco, CA, April 2000.

Wagner, C, S. Lederman and R. Howe. 2002. "A Tactile Shape Display Using RC Servomotors." http://biorobotics.harvard.edu/pubs/haptics2002_display.pdf.

Weinberg, Gili, R. Fletcher and S. Gan. 1998. "The Baby Sense Environment: Enriching and Monitoring Infants' Experiences and Communication." *Conference Summary on Human Factors in Computing Systems (CHI) '98*, pp. 325–6. New York: ACM Press.

Wisneski, C., H. Ishii, A. Dahley, M. Gorbet, S. Brave, B. Ullmer and P. Yarin. 1998. "Ambient Displays: Turning Architectural Space into an Interface between People and Digital Information." *Proceedings of International Workshop on Cooperative Buildings (CoBuild '98)*, pp. 22–32. Darmstadt: Springer Press.

Notes for Contributors

Articles should be approximately 25 pages in length and must include a three-sentence biography of the author(s) and an abstract. Interviews should not exceed 15 pages and do not require an author biography. Exhibition and book reviews are normally 500 to 2,000 words in length. The Publishers will require a disk as well as a hard copy of any contributions (please mark clearly on the disk what word-processing program has been used). Berg accepts most programs with the exception of Clarisworks.

Textile: The Journal of Cloth & Culture will produce one issue a year devoted to a single topic. Persons wishing to organize a topical issue are invited to submit a proposal which contains a hundred-word description of the topic together with a list of potential contributors and paper subjects. Proposals are accepted only after review by the journal editors and in-house editorial staff at Berg.

Manuscripts

Manuscripts should be submitted to: *Textile: The Journal of Cloth & Culture*. Manuscripts will be acknowledged by the editor and entered into the review process discussed below. Manuscripts without illustrations will not be returned unless the author provides a self-addressed stamped envelope. Submission of a manuscript to the journal will be taken to imply that it is not being considered elsewhere for publication, and that if accepted for publication, it will not be published elsewhere, in the same form, in any language, without the consent of the editor and publisher. It is a condition of acceptance by the editor of a manuscript for publication that the publishers automatically acquire the copyright of the published article throughout the world. *Textile: The Journal of Cloth & Culture* does not pay authors for their manuscripts nor does it provide retyping, drawing, or mounting of illustrations.

Style

U.S. spelling and mechanicals are to be used. Authors are advised to consult *The Chicago Manual of Style (14th Edition)* as a guideline for style. Webster's Dictionary is our arbiter of spelling. We encourage the use of major subheadings and, where appropriate, second-level subheadings. Manuscripts submitted for consideration as an article must contain: a title page with the full title of the article, the author(s) name and address, a three-sentence biography for each author, and a 200 word abstract. Do not place the author's name on any other page of the manuscript.

Manuscript Preparation

Manuscripts must be typed double-spaced (including quotations, notes, and references cited), one side only, with at least one-inch margins on standard paper using a typeface no smaller than 12pts. The original manuscript and a copy of the text on disk *(please ensure it is clearly marked with the word-processing program that has been used) must* be submitted, along with color *original* photographs (to be returned). Authors should retain a copy for their records. Any necessary artwork must be submitted with the manuscript.

Footnotes

Footnotes appear as "Notes" at the end of articles. Authors are advised to include footnote material in the text whenever possible. Notes are to be numbered consecutively throughout the paper and are to be typed double-spaced at the end of the text. (Do not use any footnoting or end-noting programs that your software may offer as this text becomes irretrievably lost at the typesetting stage.)

References

The list of references should be limited to, and inclusive of, those publications actually cited in the text. References are to be cited in the body of the text in parentheses with the author's last name, the year of original publication, and page number—e.g., (Rouch 1958: 45). Titles and publication information appear as "References" at the end of the article and should be listed alphabetically by author and chronologically for each author. Names of journals and publications should appear in full. Film and video information appears as "Filmography". References cited should be typed double-spaced on a separate page. *References not presented in the style required will be returned to the author for revision.*

Tables

All tabular material should be part of a separately numbered series of "Tables". Each table must be typed on a separate sheet and identified by a short descriptive title. Footnotes for tables appear at the bottom of the table. Marginal notations on manuscripts should indicate approximately where tables are to appear.

Figures

All illustrative material (drawings, maps, diagrams, and photographs) should be designated "Figures". They must be submitted in a form suitable for publication without redrawing. Drawings should be carefully done with black ink on either hard, white, smooth-surfaced board or good quality tracing paper. Ordinarily, computer-generated drawings are not of publishable quality. Color photographs are encouraged by the publishers. Whenever possible, photographs should be 8 × 10 inches. The publishers encourage artwork to be submitted as scanned files (300 dpi or above) on disk or via email. All figures should be clearly numbered on the back and numbered consecutively. All captions should be typed double-spaced on a separate page. Marginal notations on manuscripts should indicate approximately where figures are to appear. While the editors and publishers will use ordinary care in protecting all figures submitted, they cannot assume responsibility for their loss or damage. Authors are discouraged from submitting rare or non-replaceable materials. It is the author's responsibility to secure written copyright clearance on all photographs and drawings that are not in the public domain. Copyright should be obtained for worldwide rights and on-line publishing.

Criteria for Evaluation

Textile: The Journal of Cloth & Culture is a refereed journal. Manuscripts will be accepted only after review by both the editors and anonymous reviewers deemed competent to make professional judgments concerning the quality of the manuscript. Upon request, authors will receive reviewers' evaluations.

Reprints for Authors

Twenty-five reprints of authors' articles will be provided to the first named author free of charge. Additional reprints may be purchased upon request.

Out Now

THE ARCHITECTURE ISSUE

Contact Selvedge,
P.O Box 40038, London, N6 5UW
editor@selvedge.org
T: 0208 341 9721
www.selvedge.org

Selvedge is published 6 times a year by Selvedge Ltd